Marathon – From Beginner to Finisher

Meyer & Meyer Sport

Original title:
Compleet Handboek Looptraining. Van Joggen tot Marathon
© 2005 Zuidnederlandse Uitgeverij N.V., Aartselaar, Belgium

British Library Cataloguing in Publication Data
A catalogue record for this book is available from the British Library

Marathon – From Beginner to Finisher
Oxford: Meyer & Meyer Sport (UK) Ltd., 2007
ISBN 978-1-84126-207-9

© 2007 by Meyer & Meyer Sport (UK) Ltd.
Aachen, Adelaide, Auckland, Budapest, Graz, Johannesburg,
New York, Olten (CH), Oxford, Singapore, Toronto
Member of the World
Sports Publishers' Association (WSPA)
www.w-s-p-a.org
Printed and bound by: B.O.S.S Druck und Medien GmbH, Germany
ISBN 978-1-84126-207-9
E-Mail: verlag@m-m-sports.com
www.m-m-sports.com

Contents

Introduction

Extreme physical performances have always appealed to the imagination of a lot of people. Even today many people take up jogging to chase the ultimate dream of being able to finish a marathon one day. The 42.195 kilometer race has enjoyed a mythical, almost heroic and unattainable status for a long time.

This is in large part due to the story that supposedly created this exhausting run. According to the Greek historian Herodotus, in the year 490 BC a Greek soldier ran from Marathon to Athens to communicate the victory of the Greek army over the Persian. Upon arrival, he was only able to say "we have overcome," whereupon he dropped dead.

During the first modern Olympic games in Athens in 1896, the 40-kilometer long 'Marathon to Athens' was repeated for the first time. More than 60,000 spectators 'shouted' the Greek Louis Spiridon across the finish. In 1908 the marathon distance was officially set at 42,195 meters. This is the distance from Windsor Castle to the White City Stadium in London. The start and the finish of the running distance were chosen this way to help the the British royal family follow the race better.

The marathon also is the typical 'finale' of the Olympic Games, perhaps to welcome the real hero of the games.

The man who brought the marathon to the model jogger, or who had encouraged the average guy to jog in the first place, undoubtedly was James F. Fixx.

Fixx worked for a high profile magazine, a job which involved multiple lunches with writers as his most pleasant tasks. Once a good athlete, his weight jumped from 75 to 100 kilograms in a relatively short time and physically he was worthless. He smoked two packs of cigarettes a day and he felt more and more shamefully betrayed by his own body during his weekly tennis match.

There was but one thing he could do: live a healthier life, which would include more and more regular physical exercise as a key element. Fixx chose to go jogging. He passed through all the phases of a beginner, fought against muscular ache and inevitable injuries, stuck through it, and eventually became the running guru of the seventies. He wrote the huge best-seller "The Complete Book of Running" in which he analyzed jogging down to the smallest details and promoted jogging by enumerating its many advantages. Ironically he underwent the same fate as the Greek military messenger in Athens: Fixx died from a heart attack years later during his daily jog.

Incited by James Fixx and others, the seventies saw a gigantic jogging hype in America, and the word was out that 'marathons are for everyone.' The New York Marathon grew to be a symbol, not only for the top runners, but also for joggers from all around the world. The hype blew over to Europe, and marathons such as those of London were fully booked months in advance.

Eventually in 1984, the marathon distance was organized for women. When Gaby Anderson-Schiess, dehydrated and totally disoriented, staggered across the finish in Los Angeles, the critics of marathons for women were given their supposed "prove". It wasn't long before scientific data would prove that women are more capable than men to complete long distances.
All this obviously does not mean that jogging only offers advantages if it finally leads to running marathons. On the contrary, I am convinced that especially when preparing for a marathon, the limit of strain is far too often exceeded.
Participating in your first marathon demands long, very progressive and almost professional preparation. A marathon is feasible for almost everyone, but involves careful, gradual training.

So don't consider the marathon as the ultimate challenge, but instead think first of the unmistakable advantages jogging offers. Feel better, both mentally and physically, become fitter and more immune to stress. Adopt a more balanced lifestyle by means of jogging, and enjoy nature and the company of your running mates.

This book is here to help you reach these first objectives, to become a full-fledged runner and enable yourself to eventually and successfully start and finish a marathon. Hopefully it will also help you balance the goal of a marathon challenge with the simpler goal of attaining mental and physical health and fitness.

All subjects necessary to reach these objectives will thus be taken into consideration in this book.

How do you start jogging? Which positive impacts are brought about by regular jogging? How do you improve your condition progressively? Do you have to follow certain nutrition recommendations? Which materials do you need? How can you avoid injuries? How can you use a heartrate monitor? Which important training principles should never be overlooked?

All this will be addressed by specific training set-ups for runners of all levels.

Have a lot of 'fun running'!

CHAPTER 1

Getting started

The choice of the right running shoe

One of the great advantages of jogging is that it does not require much specific gear apart from a decent running shoe. The purchase of a quality running shoe is very important, because it will reduce the risk of injuries signaling, and is directly related to your level of running pleasure.

We must say immediately that the ideal running shoe suitable for every runner does not exist. The market is constantly being swamped with all kinds of models and technical updates. Some of these revolutionary updates disappear just as quickly as they appear, while some do stand the test of time. It has become particularly difficult to still see the forest for the trees, and the risk of a wrong purchase, causing all sorts of painful impacts, is always looming.

Anyway, a good running shoe has become rather expensive in these last few years. And although a high price is no guarantee for the quality of the shoe, it is nevertheless true that the quality must be paid for.

A running shoe must satisfy a number of uniform requirements

- **The heel cap**
  The heel cap must fix the heel firmly into the shoe. The upper part of the heel cap must be sufficiently *smooth* so that no unnecessary pressure is being placed on the Achilles tendon.
- **The sole**
  The sole must, first, be sufficiently *shock absorbing*. When running in a relaxed way the foot undergoes a strain equal to three times the body weight. This explains why heavier runners will be recommended a different type of shoe than lighter runners. Second, the sole should not be too soft, because this softness diminishes the stability of the running shoe. The sole must also be *wide* enough, and slightly bulge out at the sides. This assures greater shoe stability as it bends while running.
- **The flexibility of the sole**
  The sole must be sufficiently flexible at the point where your toes attach to the foot and bend. Too rigid soles cause enormous pressure on the sole of the foot, specifically the plantar fascia.

The individual unrolling movement of the foot

When choosing a running shoe you must take into account the individual unrolling movement of the foot. Not everyone has a normal foot, and not everyone puts their foot down the same way when running.

Putting down the foot during running happens in one of three ways:

- **Neutral**
  Putting down the foot occurs on the outside of the heel. When the complete weight comes above the foot, the foot unrolls slightly to the inside and in the direction of the large toe. This is called natural unrolling of the foot or a normal pronation, which ensures maximum shock absorption.
- **Overpronation**
  Overpronation means the runner's foot unrolls too far to the inside as a result of which the weight is absorbed by the inner ankle. The shoe sole usually will first show wearing out to the inner part of the heel. The impact is rather quickly translated into pain in the ankles, knees, hips and lower back.
- **Oversupination**
  Oversupination means the shock of putting down the foot is mainly absorbed by the outside of the foot. The foot unrolls too little to the inside. Sole wear can be determined very rapidly on the outer side of the heel. Oversupination can cause problems in the ankles, knees and the lower back.

You should also distinguish between a number of foot types:

- **The normal foot**
- **The flat foot**
  When making an impression of the wet foot sole in the ground, a flat foot will leave a print which looks like the whole sole of the foot. Runners with flat feet will overpronate in most of the cases.
- **The high-arched foot**
  When making an impression of the wet foot sole in the ground, a high-arched foot will leave a print showing a very narrow band or no band at all between the forefoot and the heel. High-arched feet create oversupination in most cases.

When a runners foot deviates greatly from the normal foot, an existing shoe type will not be sufficient. Possible solutions are introducing adaptations to the shoe itself, or having individually adapted insoles made.

TIP:
Choose a running shoe suitable for your individual running profile. Let a specialist give you advice. When you suspect you have a deviating running profile, get counseling by means of a biomechanical analysis on the treadmill.

The 'wearing out' profile

You can determine quite a lot from the wearing out profile of the heel of an old running shoe that will help you choose a new shoe.

For a neutral foot we see wear to the outside of the heel. This is normal because the outer parts of the heel are put down first when running. Furthermore we see even, symmetrical wear to the front of the foot, because you push away with a flat front foot.

In the case of oversupination, we see strong wear on the outer side of the sole, not only at the heel, but also to the front because you push off with the outside of your foot. In the case of overpronation, it is the inner part of the entire sole which shows wear.

Heavier runners would best choose a heavier, firm shoe with good shock absorption, even when running races. This is perhaps slightly contrary to your gut feeling. Lighter shoes are attractive, but generally they will increase your risk of overuse injuries. Specific race shoes are very light, often scarcely 300 grams, but they have significantly less impact strength and give less support. That is why they not recommended for use during training, even when high-tempo training sessions should be completed.

The correct shoe size

The correct shoe size is, of course, very important too. Too small shoes lead to a cramped running style, and they cause painful, blue toenails before you know it. After some time these toenails get loose and eventually drop off. Too large shoes will quickly cause blisters, due to the constant movement of the foot in the shoe.

Running shoes should be rather tight at the side of the heel, so they provide stability to the heel and the ankle. The front foot should be rather broad and provide plenty of room.

The life span of running shoes

The life span of running shoes depends on:

- **The quality of the shoe** – shoes of a high quality will last longer.

- **The surface of the training track** on hard surfaces, shoes will wear out much sooner than when training on a soft surface.

- **The running style** – runners with a normal running profile will be able to run longer with the same shoes than runners with a deviating running profile (overpronation or oversupination).

- **The care which is given to the shoes after a training session** – Your shoes should be completely dry and you should remove all remaining mud before running again. It is best to have two pairs of running shoes, so that you can alternate for every other training session.

Following these guidelines will allow good training running shoes to last up to 1000 kilometers (600 miles). Your race shoes obviously have a much shorter life span. You can see wear to the lower part of the sole in particular, which means the mid sole, which ensures most of the shock absorption, is so worn out that there is an urgent need to buy new shoes.

TIP:

Buy preferably two pairs of running shoes and switch for every training session. Never run with worn-out shoes.

Running attire

Running in warm and dry conditions

Once you have chosen correct, individually adapted running shoes, the most difficult and most important work concerning equipment is done. Especially during warmer months, there are few concerns about your running gear. Without any problems, you can jog in an old cotton T-shirt and shorts. Make sure they are loose enough, but it is also very important that the T-shirt does not rub against the nipples during running. This can lead to very painful scrape wounds.

With running shorts as well, be careful to avoid scrape wounds to the inner side of the thighs.

TIP:

Persons with thicker upper legs, which rub against one another during running, preferably opt for thin short stretch pants, similar to cycling pants.

Of course, there is a complete range of specific running attire available, and it definitely raises the comfort level for runners. This new attire contains artificial fibers which are much lighter, and which brings the sweat to the outside of the shirt, so it can evaporate quickly. That is why sweat will dry much faster in these new fabrics than in a cotton T-shirt.

Socks are generally made of cotton, which ensures that your feet remain dry. An important requirement is that the socks fit well, and do not fall into folds during running. Painful blisters will be the inevitable consequence.

Some runners prefer jogging bare chested in summer temperatures. You should avoid this. Your skin absorbs all the heat, which causes your body temperature to increase too dramatically. If you run in the sun, you should protect your body by wearing a white, thin T-shirt. This will reflect the sunbeams.

Running in cold and wet conditions

In cold and wet conditions the demands made on the running attire are a lot more serious. You can run in the rain or in freezing conditions, but you must take into account a number of things.

First of all, you must remain dry. There is nothing worse for a runner that to cool down whilerunning in the rain. In rainy weather you should wear a light rain jacket that meets three requirements: it must be windproof, water resistant, and must breathe. Breathing means that the sweat can evaporate through the jacket. If this is not the case you will quickly perspire under your jacket. Then there is a risk that your body temperature will increase too drastically.

Never wear too many clothes, even if it is cold. Two to three rather thin layers are generally enough, and it is better to wear a couple of thin layers than wearing one thick layer.

TIP:

Apply reflecting strips to your running attire, especially if you run at night. Most rain jackets are equipped with these strips. If you run often in the dark it is also advisable to add strips to your shoes (sides and back) and possibly to your running pants as well.

In cold and wet weather you need to keep your muscles warm. Running in long pants is an absolute must. Loose cotton training pants should suffice, in dry and cold weather in particular.

Tightly fitting running pants raise comfort, however. They are of course much lighter, and they allow much better vaporization of sweat. Make sure these pants are very smooth so they do not obstruct the stretching and bending movement in the knee joint. There are also running pants which are especially devised for running in rainy weather. To the front they are equipped with a water resistant layer.

A lot of body warmth is lost via the head. Therefore it is advisable to put a bonnet on your head when it is cold, and in freezing conditions you should certainly cover your ears. Here again, you can choose between a cotton bonnet and a 'breathing' bonnet especially devised for runners. In rainy weather a cap is no superfluous luxury. In the summer as well, it is pleasant to wear a light cap as protection against the sun.

When it freezes, make sure you have gloves at your disposal and then you are ready to feel good during jogging in all kinds of weather conditions!

TIP:

Choose adapted running attire especially in cold and wet conditions. You will feel more comfortable, and running will become a pleasant experience in all weather conditions.

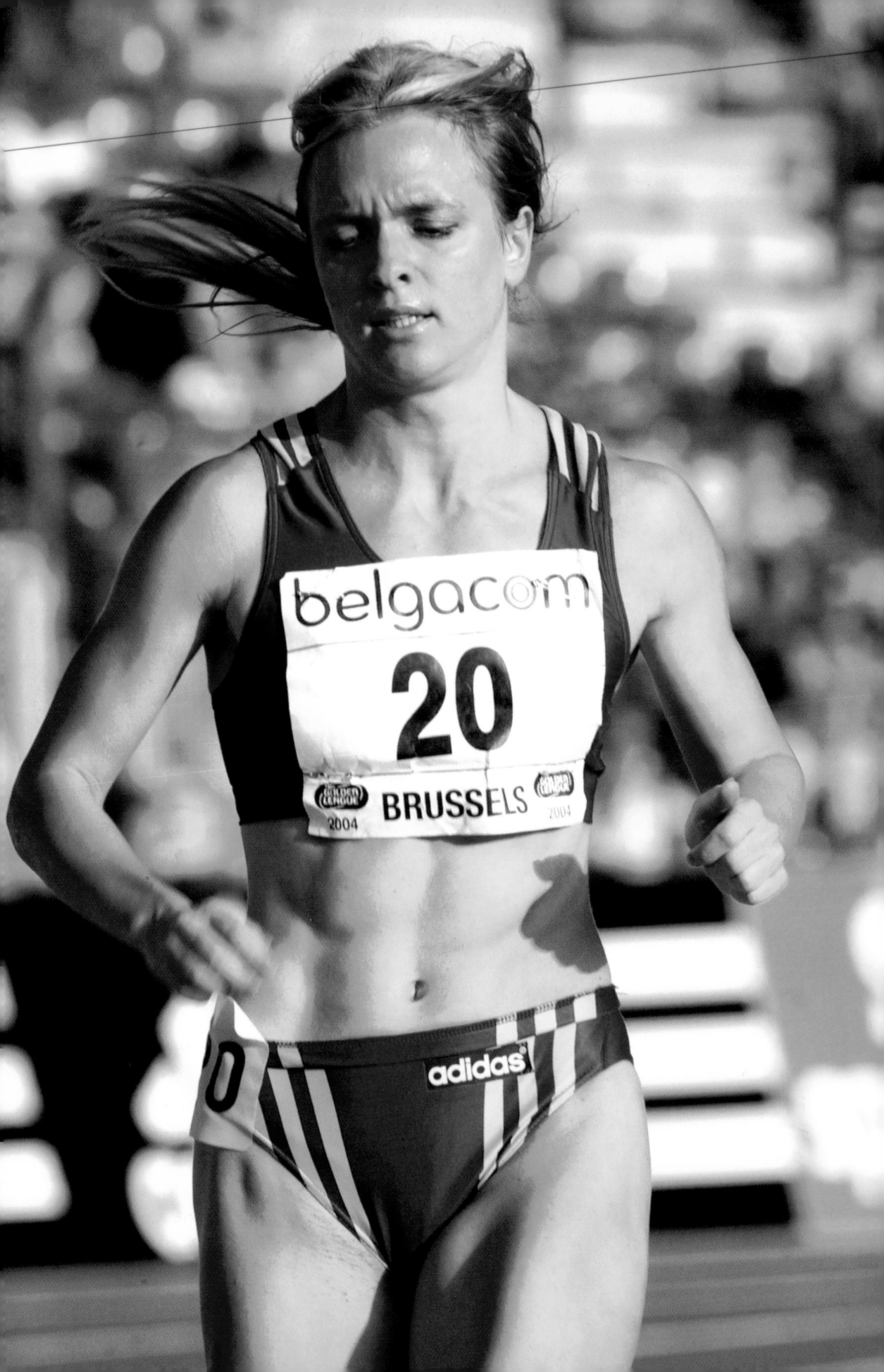
belgacom
20
BRUSSELS
2004
2004
adidas

CHAPTER 2

The advantages of a running program

Running is a fantastic sport, which will undoubtedly offer you lots of advantages in the short term – mentally, physically and socially. You can jog almost everywhere at every moment of the day, and even if you start from scratch, you will be able to attain a level that will give you great satisfaction. Running meets one of the most fundamental needs of mankind, namely the need to move, freely, without any material support. Running – just as a fish swims, and a bird flies.

The physical advantages

For a long time people have been convinced that regular, moderate exercise has a positive influence on the physical well-being of people, and that endurance sports have a direct or indirect positive impact on life span.

This influence manifests itself in multiple ways – in the cardiovascular area at the level of the heart and blood cycle, in the category of a better processing of fat, and finally in a strengthening of the immune system.

Better functioning of the heart and blood cycle

Regular jogging ensures good training of the heart, allowing the heart to function more efficiently and more economically.

The heart is a muscle. When a muscle is stimulated by doing endurance sports, it becomes stronger and larger. This enlarging is more specifically caused by an increase of the heart volume, and not by the thickening of the heart partition. The latter occurs more often because of the multiple implementations of short-term, intensive efforts.

This increase of the heart volume means the heart fills more after each contraction, and as a result, more blood can be pumped to the outside at the next contraction. This results in better oxygen transport to the working muscles at each heartbeat. That is why the heart rate at rest decreases as one is better trained, and the heart rate remains at a lower level after an identical effort. The efficiency of the heart functioning therefore increases considerably.

The working muscles will be better blooded in general. New veins are being formed around these muscles, allowing blood to be provided more efficiently. Because of this, the oxygen transport in the body improves.

Better processing of fat

Jogging also has a very positive influence on the processing of the visible and invisible fat in your body.

First of all, the cholesterol quantity in the blood decreases. Cholesterol is a type of fat that circulates in your blood. When you eat too much fatty food, cholesterol quantity increases. This cholesterol is, in the long term, responsible for the veins literally "silting up." When the veins which provide the heart with blood get silted, a heart infarction occurs, often with fatal impact.

Secondly, the body oxidizes fat more efficiently. Fat oxidizing enzymes will be produced, and the body will make longer and better use of the oxidation of fat in the energy supply of the body. Even after training the body keeps on processing fat.

TIP:
Keep the intensity of training low if you want to burn fat. If you do sports intensively you will mainly burn carbohydrates.

Strengthening of the immune system

With moderate exercise your immune system is reinforced. This means that you become less subject to infections, such as colds. Colds are the consequence of contact with certain viruses. It is impossible not to come in contact with these viruses, which are spread by sneezing, coughing, ordinary breathing or shaking hands with a contaminated person. If your defense system against these viruses is weak, you have a greater chance to get contaminated. That is why it is essential to reinforce your resistance against these viruses. Research has shown that moderate exercise has a positive impact on the functioning of the immune system. But if you exhaust yourself by very intensive training sessions, you create an opposite impact – it will backfire and you will become more liable for all kinds of infections.

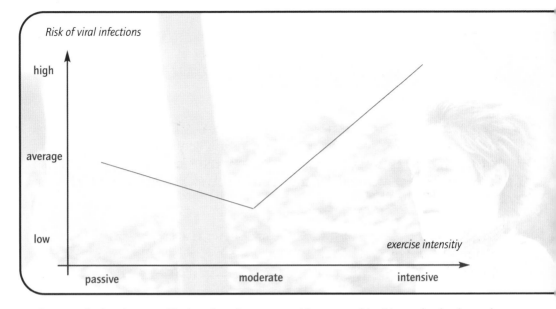

If you train hard, you will therefore be more subject to colds. Not only the intensive training sessions, but the races also have a negative influence on the immune system. The cause of this is not only to be found in the physical stress which the body undergoes, but also in the mental stress. If you are stressed, you have a greater risk of colds than if you are mentally relaxed.

Moreover the immune system is also weakened by sudden cooling down after training and races.

TIP:

Put on dry clothes as soon as possible after a training session or a race to prevent cooling down suddenly.

There are still a number of other advantages gained by running. Because of the shocks during running, the firmness of your bones will increase. Especially for women, this will reduce the risk of osteoporosis. The ageing process is slowed down and general fitness increases. Finally, a run training session demands little time. It can easily be practiced whenever it fits into your day, and is therefore particularly suitable for busy people.

Preventive measures

In spite of these unmistakable advantages, it is important to realize that this sport demands much of your body – especially at an early stage, but also later, when the volume and the intensity are forced up over time.

A preventive visit to the doctor is recommended before you start your jogging career, especially when one or more of the following apply to you:

- you have never done sports or you have been inactive for a number of years,
- you are corpulent,
- you smoke or recently quit,
- you suffer from dizziness,
- your chest aches during physical effort,
- you have heart disease, or there is a history of heart disease in your family
- you suffer from shortness of breath,
- you have been taking medicines for an extended period.

It is rarely the case that your doctor will prohibit you to jog, but he may place intensity restrictions on you. Obey the recommendations of your doctor under all circumstances.

TIP:

Never ignore pain indicators during running. Contact a doctor when you suffer from shortness of breath, chest pain or dizziness during jogging.

The mental advantages

The insight in the mid-seventies that body movement brings along many physical advantages was completed by the idea that endurance sports such as running, cycling and swimming have a favorable mental impact as well.

Running therapy

In 1974, Dr. Kostrubala, head of the psychiatric department of the Mercy Hospital in San Diego, launched a study into the physiological and psychological advantages of endurance exercise, such as walking and running, among the students at San Diego State University. The results were such that he decided to develop running therapy for his patients. He described this therapy in 1976, in his book "The Joy of Running". Patients who chose this deviation from the traditional therapy combined an hour of running or walking training two to four times per week (once with a therapist) with an hour of group therapy. During the training session, much attention was given to physical sensations.

The results of this new therapy were called "spectacular." People who suffered from a depression as a result of problems at work, in the family or due to other psychological problems obtained, among other things, a lower heart rate at rest and during effort. Their blood pressure decreased, their fat oxidation increased, and their cholesterol levels decreased.

In the psychological area, their feelings of fear reduced while their feeling of well-being was being raised. They obtained better control over their daily stressors and raised their tolerance for these stressors.

TIP:

In a stressful period, it is always important to spare some time to jog. This can even have a positive influence on important decisions.

A healthy mind in a healthy body

A healthy mind in a healthy body (mens sana in corpore sano) is a wisdom first proclaimed at the time of the Romans. The beneficial functioning of body movement on mental well-being is therefore clearly no recent revelation.

Exercise for many people means rediscovering your own body, going through experiences almost forgotten. The balance between body and mind is renewed.

Regaining certain basic conditioning has a satisfactory impact. At a later stage this will provide the people who stick with running a stronger feeling of self-worth. Being a fit person you can do more and you look better, and your self-respect gets a boost as a result. The regained fitness enhances a generally healthier life style.

Sports can break through the daily rut, certainly when you exercise in a group. The social contact often has a relaxing impact.

Endorphins

The main reason exercise helps suppress stress and, at a later stage, depression, is due to the so-called endorphins being produced during the effort.

Endorphins are morphine-like substances produced by the body itself. They act like an internal kind of drug. The resemblance with morphine explains why a runner could be feeling "high" during endurance training. In extreme cases this feeling is even described as "things becoming much clearer," and still at a later stage, that "colors and forms overflow." After a deliciously relaxing running session it is sometimes impossible to exactly reconstruct the route taken.

Because of the endorphins produced, it is possible that endurance sports have an addictive impact in the long term, not only mentally, but also physically. After some time the body is so used to the effort and the endorphins that all kinds of physical responses can arise, such as palpitations, when you don't engage in any sports for a long time. Therefore professional sportsmen are, for example, strongly dissuaded to abruptly stop training after the competitive period or after ending their careers. We all need a detox phase, during which the sportsman cuts down his training gradually.

The theory about the endorphins sounds, of course, very tempting. What kind of experience is more beautiful than the blissful impact of an activity which has only positive influence on the body, both physically and mentally? Why isn't everyone an enthusiastic jogger?

Before transferring into the addictive phase of the endurance sport, the starting jogger must struggle through a period characterized by pain, sadness and torment. The passive body, which has suffered through years of poor and excessive nutrition, exuberant alcohol consumption and fatal smoking behavior, must suddenly adapt to all the demands being made on active people. Everything cracks and squeaks, the expiration date of the joints has perhaps been already exceeded due to inactivity, and the contents of the engine hardly exceed half a cylinder. Overuse injuries, even at apparently restricted exercise intensity, will always be lurking around the corner.

CHAPTER 3

Beginning!

Jogging is an excellent sport with numerous physical and mental benefits. Besides these benefits, we must also mention that jogging is a rather hard sport that has no mercy to everyone who has too little physical condition.

The impact of this sport on your body is immediate and very intense: your breathing rhythm is already forced up from the first running steps, your body temperature increases immediately and your tendons, joints and muscles must endure unusual pressure from the very start.

This means your body needs a certain adaptation period before you can experience any real pleasure in this sport.

This adaptation period depends on a number of factors:

* *Your body weight:* for heavier persons the impact of running on the body will be greater.

* *Your initial condition:* the better your initial condition, the sooner you will experience running as a pleasant leisure activity.

* *The regularity of the training sessions:* if there is too much time between training sessions, the positive impact of the previous training is lost.

* *Your motivation:* if you are motivated you will be able to endure the impact of running better. Motivation can be reinforced by doing as much running as possible in the company of one or more other runners. However, you cannot lose sight of the fact that you must still find your own intrinsic motivation; this means that there must be a positive driving force which comes from within yourself.

Important guidelines

The risk of overload injuries cannot be underestimated. Painful joints, tendinitis in knees and feet and a painful lower back are never far away for those who throw themselves into this sport too enthusiastically and fanatically.

For this reason you must take into account a number of specific guidelines:

- Run preferably on a soft surface. This offers significantly more shock absorption than if you run on asphalt or on concrete.

- Begin at a very low level in running intensity and training volume. Initially, force up the running volume very gradually and only think about forcing up tempo later. A volume increase of approximately 15% per week is more than enough.

- Count the training volume in minutes, not in kilometers.

- Stop immediately if you feel any pain. Only begin again if you can run without pain.

- Seek advice from an expert when buying running shoes. Not every shoe is suitable for every runner. Sometimes an adaptation to the shoe is needed or special insoles should be made to correct certain deviations in feet, knees or pelvis.

- If you must interrupt running training because of illness or injury, always begin again at a level lower than where you left off.

Your first running set-up

The aim of the running set-up below is to be able to jog four times per week for 30 minutes at a very quiet tempo after 9 weeks.
The way the first training sessions are carried out is of vital importance to the success of this program.

For this reason the following is important:

- Strictly stick to the training volume, even if you feel like you can already process more.

- Run very slowly, and combine the running phases with walking during the first weeks.

- Run to such a tempo that enables you to never be out of breath during jogging, and that you are always able to talk during the effort.

Week 1

We start with three training sessions of 15 minutes during the first week. This seems little, but to avoid overload this is enough. Run very slowly, and constantly switch between running and walking.

Day	Activity
Monday	Walking-jogging: 15 minutes alternatively jogging and walking. Alternation happens instinctively. The walking time can exceed the running time. Light stretching after the effort
Tuesday	Recovery day
Wednesday	Recovery day
Thursday	Walking-jogging: 15 minutes alternatively jogging and walking. Alternation happens instinctively. Light stretching after the effort
Friday	Recovery day
Saturday	Walking-jogging: 15 minutes alternatively jogging and walking. Alternation happens instinctively. Light stretching after the effort
Sunday	Recovery day

TOTAL	45 minutes walking-jogging
Estimated calorie use/week	300 kcal

Week 2

Overall walking-jogging-time is forced up to 51 minutes during this week. This means an increase of approximately 15%.

You will undoubtedly see yourself having improved. The tempo remains very slow, but try to cut down the walking time within the same training session, and therefore extend the jogging time. But do not overstrain yourself. Immediately start walking when you are getting tired.

Day	Activity
Monday	Walking-jogging: 17 minutes alternatively jogging and walking. Alternation happens instinctively. The walking time can exceed the running time. Light stretching after the effort
Tuesday	Recovery day
Wednesday	Recovery day
Thursday	Walking-jogging: 17 minutes alternatively jogging and walking. Alternation happens instinctively. The walking time can exceed the running time. Light stretching after the effort
Friday	Recovery day
Saturday	Walking-jogging: 17 minutes alternatively jogging and walking. Alternation happens instinctively. The walking time can exceed the running time. Light stretching after the effort
Sunday	Recovery day
TOTAL Estimated calorie use/week	51 minutes walking-jogging + stretching 400 kcal

Week 3

At the end of the third week overall walking-jogging-time must be approximately 60 minutes. This is about fifteen per cent more than last week.

The task is still the same as last week: do not only force up the total time, but also the running time with respect to the walking time. Pay attention to your breathing: you should never be short of breath.

Day	Activity
Monday	Walking-jogging: 20 minutes alternatively jogging and walking. Alternation happens instinctively. The walking time can exceed the running time. Light stretching after the effort
Tuesday	Recovery day
Wednesday	Recovery day
Thursday	Walking-jogging: 20 minutes alternatively jogging and walking. Alternation happens instinctively. The walking time can exceed the running time. Light stretching after the effort
Friday	Recovery day
Saturday	Walking-jogging: 20 minutes alternatively jogging and walking. Alternation happens instinctively. The walking time can exceed the running time. Light stretching after the effort
Sunday	Recovery day
TOTAL Estimated calorie use/week	60 minutes walking-jogging + stretching 500 kcal

Week 4

At the end of this fourth week you will have trained 69 minutes, but you should still progress very gradually. Keep on running very slowly, and interrupt running by walking breaks just like during the previous weeks.

These walking breaks must, however, become shorter and shorter. Gradually we get ready to carry out training sessions involving constant running.

Day	Activity
Monday	Walking-jogging: 23 minutes alternatively jogging and walking. Alternation happens instinctively. The walking time can exceed the running time. Light stretching after the effort
Tuesday	Recovery day
Wednesday	Recovery day
Thursday	Walking-jogging: 23 minutes alternatively jogging and walking. Alternation happens instinctively. The walking time can exceed the running time. Light stretching after the effort
Friday	Recovery day
Saturday	Walking-jogging: 23 minutes alternatively jogging and walking. Alternation happens instinctively. The walking time can exceed the running time. Light stretching after the effort
Sunday	Recovery day
TOTAL Estimated calorie use/Week	69 minutes walking-jogging + stretching 570 kcal

Week 5

During this fifth week we go from three to four running sessions. This way we reach a total volume of 80 minutes.

During the additional session of 15 minutes you must try to always keep on running. The tempo can and must remain very low. During the other sessions the running time must now exceed the walking time.

Day	Activity
Monday	Walking-jogging: 20 minutes alternatively jogging and walking. Alternation happens instinctively. The running time can exceed the walking time. Light stretching after the effort
Tuesday	Jogging: 15 minutes continuous jogging at easy tempo
Wednesday	Recovery day
Thursday	Walking-jogging: 25 minutes alternatively jogging and walking. Alternation happens instinctively. The walking time can exceed the running time. Light stretching after the effort
Friday	Recovery day
Saturday	Walking-jogging: 20 minutes alternatively jogging and walking. Alternation happens instinctively. The walking time can exceed the running time. Light stretching after the effort
Sunday	Recovery day
TOTAL Estimated calorie use/week	80 minutes walking-jogging and jogging + stretching 660 kcal

Week 6

In week 6 you take a great leap forward.

The overall training time (90 minutes) now already amounts to twice the time of the first week, and during two training sessions of 20 minutes you run constantly, very slowly. During the other running training sessions, running is still alternated with walking.

Day	Activity
Monday	Walking-jogging: 25 minutes alternatively jogging and walking. Alternation happens instinctively. The walking time can exceed the running time. Light stretching
Tuesday	Jogging: 20 minutes jogging continuously at easy tempo Light stretching
Wednesday	Recovery day
Thursday	Jogging: 20 minutes jogging continuously at easy tempo. Light stretching
Friday	Recovery day
Saturday	Walking-jogging: 25 minutes alternatively jogging and walking. Alternation happens instinctively. Light stretching
Sunday	Recovery day
TOTAL Estimated calorie use/week	90 minutes walking-jogging and jogging + stretching 750 kcal

Week 7

The aim of this program is to be able to run continuously four times per week for 30 minutes within a period of nine weeks. You should still go through a continual progression during the remaining three weeks.

During the previous six weeks a sufficient basis must have been built to proceed to three ongoing running sessions, which includes one of 30 minutes.
The overall training time is 105 minutes at the end of this week. Try jogging continuously during 20 minutes during two training sessions.
Do the same during a 30 minute session.

Alternate between running and walking during the remaining training session.

Day	Activity
Monday	Jogging: 30 minutes jogging continuously at easy tempo Light stretching
Tuesday	Jogging: 20 minutes jogging continuously at easy tempo Light stretching
Wednesday	Recovery day
Thursday	Jogging: 20 minutes trying to jog continuously at easy tempo Light stretching
Friday	Recovery day
Saturday	Walking-jogging: 35 minutes alternatively jogging and walking. Alternation happens instinctively. Light stretching
Sunday	Recovery day
TOTAL Estimated calorie use/week	105 minutes walking-jogging and jogging + stretching 880 kcal

Week 8

The overall training time is this week 120 minutes (+ 15%). 30 minutes jogging continuously during two sessions and 25 minutes during another session.
After this week you are ready to reach the goal set in advance.

Day	Activity
Monday	Jogging: 30 minutes jogging continuously at easy tempo Light stretching
Tuesday	Jogging: 25 minutes jogging continuously at easy tempo Light stretching
Wednesday	Recovery day
Thursday	Jogging: 30 minutes jogging continuously at easy tempo Light stretching
Friday	Recovery day
Saturday	Walking-jogging: 35 minutes alternatively jogging and walking. Alternation happens instinctively. Light stretching
Sunday	Recovery day
TOTAL Estimated calorie use/week	120 minutes walking-jogging and jogging + stretching 1000 kcal

Week 9

The overall training time must no longer be forced up. Progress is obvious in the fact that you do not walk during any of the four training sessions.

Day	Activity
Monday	Jogging: 30 minutes jogging continuously at easy tempo Light stretching
Tuesday	Jogging: 30 minutes jogging continuously at easy tempo Light stretching
Wednesday	Recovery day
Thursday	Jogging: 30 minutes jogging continuously at easy tempo Light stretching
Friday	Recovery day
Saturday	Jogging: 30 minutes jogging continuously at easy tempo Light stretching
Sunday	Recovery day
TOTAL estimated calorie use/week	120 minutes jogging + stretching 1100 kcal

The progress you have made in comparison to the first training week can be considered spectacular. If you are able to jog 30 minutes four times per week, albeit to slow tempo, your degree of fitness has reached a more than acceptable level.

s without any problems

...e able to run four times 30 minutes without any problems, you
... more. You are ready for more, as well. Your body has already undergone
quite a change during the past nine weeks.

In the diagram below, the training volume is forced up during the first four weeks. The
running pace remains slow. The progress is built up by means of the increasing block-system
cycle (see later), hence that the training volume during the fourth week is scaled back.

	Week 1	Week 2	Week 3	Week 4
Monday				
Tuesday	30 min T1	35 min T1	35 min T1	30 min T1
Wednesday				
Thursday	35 min T1	40 min T1	45 min T1	35 min T1
Friday				
Saturday	35 min T1	45 min T1	50 min T1	35 min T1
Sunday	30 min T1	30 min T1	30 min T1	30 min T1
TOTAL	130 min	150 min	160 min	130 min

T1 = very slow running pace, never out of breath, always able to talk

TIP:
Do not stick to your running diagram at any cost. You interrupt training planning
immediately if ill or injured, and afterwards resume training at a lower level.

During the following five weeks the running pace is now and then slightly forced up.
Because of this you will gradually be able to run to a higher tempo, and your endurance
limit will rise. You will also be able to run 60 minutes continuously at the end of this period.

Nevertheless it is still essential that you never be out of breath. You should always keep
the feeling that the effort can be continued without too many problems, and longer
than the time provided.

	Week 5	Week 6	Week 7	Week 8	Week 9
Monday					
Tuesday	35 min T2	45 min T2	40 min T2	30 min T2	30 min T2
Wednesday					
Thursday	50 minT1	55 min T1	60 min T1	45 min T1	60 min T1
Friday					
Saturday	15 min T1	15 minT1	15 min T1	15 min T3	10 min T1
	10 min T3	15 min T1	20 min T3	15 min T3	2x15 min T3
	15 min T1	10 min T1	10 min T1	10 min T1	rec. 3 min T1
					15 min T1
Sunday	30 min T1	35 min T1	35 min T1	30 min T1	40 min T1
TOTAL	155 min	175 min	180 min	145 min	185 min

T1 = very slow running pace
T2 = somewhat faster than T1, but still feeling comfortable
T3 = faster than T2, less comfortable feeling, talking becomes more difficult

CHAPTER 4

The different types of training

If you can run ten kilometers without interruption, you probably want more. Perhaps you are dreaming of completing half a marathon, or perhaps even a complete marathon. To still be able to progress you need to bring more variation into your running program.

Energy supply of the body

To get a better idea on the different training options available, you need to obtain a correct insight in the energy supply of the body.

We can consider the body as a constantly working engine. To keep this engine going you always need to have enough fuel. Our body needs several types of fuel, and which kind depends on the duration and the intensity of the effort..

Energy for the short and intense efforts

A restricted quantity of energy has been stockpiled in our body in the form of ATP (adenosinetriphosphate) and CP (creatine phosphate). This energy is immediately available, but is consumed after just a few seconds. If the effort lasts longer than a few seconds, another energy supply must be used, namely glycogen. These are carbohydrates which pile up in the muscles and the liver. If the effort is intense, and lasts for quite some time, then lactic acid forms in the muscles. The piling-up of lactic acid presents you with a blocking feeling in your muscles and forces you to either stop the effort or at least scale back the intensity drastically.

This feeling is very intense, for example, when you run 400m all out. After 300 meters not only do your legs hurt, but your arms start feeling extremely heavy. The muscles are completely full of lactic acid and it becomes impossible, in spite of all will power, to continue running at the same pace.

The utilization of the above mentioned energy sources takes place without the mediation of oxygen. Therefore this is called **anaerobic energy supply.**

Energy for long-term efforts to low intensity

When the effort lasts longer at a lower intensity, the body continues to appeal partially to the oxidation of carbohydrates. But on the other hand, and this is interesting, the body depends to a great extent on the oxidation of fatty acids.

The big difference between energy for long-term, low intensity efforts and the energy supply for short-term, high intensity efforts is that the amount of energy now available is much larger and therefore much more slowly consumed. This kind of energy is provided with mediation of oxygen. We call this **aerobic energy supply**.

The two largest energy sources are therefore fatty acids and carbohydrates. Which of these two energy sources will be utilized by the body depends first on the intensity of the effort.

For a low intensity, long-term effort energy will mainly be provided by oxidation of fatty acids. When the intensity of the effort rises, the share of carbohydrate oxidation will increase. If the carbohydrate supply is sufficient, it can provide energy for approximately 90 minutes. Its stock is therefore relatively limited. After a while the body must switch to oxidation of fatty acids.

The feeling which comes along with this change of energy supply by carbohydrates to energy supply by fatty acids is experienced as the infamous – "punch of the hammer" or as "encountering the wall."

This is caused by the fact that for the same quantity oxygen taken in, fatty acids release less energy than carbohydrates. The moment when your carbohydrates are consumed, you suddenly obtain, without warning, less energy. This feels like having extremely heavy legs.

The fat store in the body is seemingly inexhaustible. When a runner is well trained for long distances he will still be able to utilize this fat supply for a higher effort because oxidation is more efficient than for untrained runners. In other words, a well-trained athlete can make his carbohydrate supply last longer, whereas a beginner starts consuming his carbohydrates much sooner.

A good aerobic endurance capacity mainly serves efforts of relatively low intensity and long duration. "Relatively" indicates that the athlete's degree of training must be taken into account. Low intensity for a well-trained athlete could mean high intensity for a beginner.

Conclusion:

The energy source utilized in our body during physical efforts depends on:

- The intensity of the effort
- The duration of the effort
- The situation stipulated by nutrition (extra glycogen in the body)
- The degree of being trained

Various types of training

Recovery training

Recovery training is carried out to recover from preceding training sessions. The intensity is very low, and the training volume limited. These training sessions have a favorable impact on removing the waste products in the muscles and they are generally preferred to passive recovery.

The importance of the recovery training cannot be underestimated. You should train hard in order to obtain results, but the eventual training impact can only be realized during the (active) recovery period.

A real recovery training session never lasts longer than 30 to 45 minutes. It depends on your degree of fitness. If, for example, you run more than 45 minutes, you cannot consider this being recovery training, even for well-trained people. This should be looked upon as endurance training.

Aerobic endurance training

The perfect means to improve **aerobic endurance capacity** is aerobic endurance training. As mentioned before, this kind of endurance is *the* basic physical characteristic a distance runner should develop because it mobilizes the fat supply. Aerobic endurance training also forms the basis for all other more intensive training sessions.

The aerobic endurance capacity is often indicated by the **maximal oxygen uptake (VO$_2$max)**. This parameter indicates how much oxygen can be incorporated in the muscle fibers (mainly the active muscles) of the athlete at maximum effort. **VO$_2$max**, considered absolutely, is expressed in liters per minute. Because a very muscular athlete can take in more oxygen (considered absolutely) than a light athlete with less muscle mass, VO_2max is divided by the weight and is expressed in ml./min/kilogram. This is the relative capacity of oxygen uptake. High VO_2max indicates a large capacity to oxidize energy supplies (carbohydrates and fatty acids). This is of course favorable to making long-term efforts. Measuring the maximum capacity of oxygen intake is rather time-consuming and provides no absolute value judgment concerning the aerobic capacity of the athlete. However, it is common belief that VO_2max of 60ml/min.kg is a base requirement to achieve good results as a distance runner.

Aerobic endurance training can be subdivided into three levels:
Aerobic Endurance Training level 1 (AET1), Aerobic Endurance Training level 2 (AET2) and Aerobic Endurance Training level 3 (AET3).

- **AET1**, also known as Long Slow Distance (LSD), is very important for an athlete. These are training sessions which last a very long time, generally longer than a race. The pace is relatively low, so you can easily chat during training. Energy is mainly provided by oxidation of fatty acids.

- In **AET2** the training pace also remains relatively low, but somewhat higher than in the LSD. Although oxidation of fatty acids is still essential for energy supply, the share of oxidation of carbohydrates increases. By means of this type of training the athlete prepares himself for the more intensive training coming.

The AET1 and AET2 are very important because they will allow the athlete to run at a higher pace on the basis of the fat metabolism, meaning running without the carbohydrate store being utilized.

- **AET3** sessions are shorter than the AET1 and AET2 sessions and the intensity is significantly higher. The athlete has a less comfortable feeling, breathing rhythm is quicker and talking becomes more difficult.

    This training takes place in the area under the threshold (see further), and has a positive influence on the carbohydrate metabolism. By means of these high intensity endurance training sessions, the endurance limit is being moved, i.e. you can run at a higher speed for a longer time without lactic acid piling up.

    An AET3 session generally lasts 20 to a maximum of 45 minutes, apart from warm up and cool down time. As the race season approaches, the AET3 sessions will gain importance. Their share should never account for more than 10 to 20% of the total training volume.

Fartlek

Fartlek can be considered a form of interval training. Interval training is a training principle in which strain and recovery are systematically varied. In a fartlek, this alternation takes place instinctively. You will while playing, for example taking into account the nature of the track, build in rhythm changes during your training.

Whether you are training to improve your aerobic or the anaerobic endurance depends on the intensity of the high intensity segments.

HINT:

Fartlek is a playful and pleasant way to train for endurance. For a distance runner, training to improve aerobic endurance is quintessential. Therefore you must make sure that the intensity of this training session is not too high.

Tempo interval training

Doing the tempo interval run means you run a part of the distance of the upcoming race at a tempo equal to or faster than the race tempo. These distances are repeated, with a short recovery period in between which only allows incomplete recovery.

If you are, for example, capable of running 10 kilometers in 40 minutes (4 minutes a kilometer), you will run 8 times 1000 meters at a speed of 3:55-4 minutes. Between the repetitions you run 200 to 400 meters very relaxed.

High intensity interval training

High intensity interval training is the perfect way to improve **anaerobic endurance capacity.** High intensity interval training actually teaches the body to cope with this lactic acid so that its piling-up is better endured. The anaerobic endurance capacity is therefore very important for efforts of high intensity and short duration.
This base characteristic is best trained by doing successive short-term efforts (30 sec to 90 sec) at very high, even maximum intensity. The number of repetitions is low (3 to 5 times) and the pause between the successive efforts is incomplete, so that the lactic acid has not been removed entirely when the next effort is started.

These are very tough training sessions that demand much of you. You do not get many benefits from training this type of endurance, because these training sessions, if carried out too often, will have a negative impact on your aerobic endurance.

That is why you can only attempt this type of training, assuming you are well trained, if and only if the volume of these training sessions is limited to 2 to 5 % of the total training volume.

Note: the threshold

The term "threshold" causes quite a lot of confusion. The term threshold implies a heart rate which borders both the aerobic and the anaerobic energy supply level. Threshold training means training in the aerobic-anaerobic area. These training sessions are very effective to extend stamina, i.e. being able to perform without "going into the red".

Threshold cannot be confused with maximal lactate steady-state. Maximal lactate steady-state refers to the maximal effort intensity which can be maintained without any lactic acid being detected in the blood during the effort.

CHAPTER 5

Determining training intensity

The key to improving the performance level lies in pairing the type of training you want to pursue with the right training intensity.

In other words, if you want to carry out LSD (AET1) training, you must know exactly how fast (or how slow) you can run to realize the training impact you want from this kind of training. This type of training specifically aims to stimulate oxidation of fatty acids, among other things. Too high a tempo would, however, stimulate carbohydrate oxidation, instead.

In addition, determining the right training intensity is important to stipulating the time needed to reach supercompensation (see below).

You should pay attention to both the quantity of training and the quality (intensity) of training. This intensity can vary, from vaguely to very detailed. You can define the quality of a training session as quiet, extensive, recovery training, fartlek, intensive, etc.

You can also express the training intensity using figures, e.g. "up to 80% of maximum", "12 kilometers per hour", "to a heart rate between 170 and 175", or "doing a tempo of more or less 2 mmol lactic acid".

Obviously the closer the training intensity and the efficiency come to overlapping, the more effective the training will be.

Generally speaking the most common parameters used to define the training intensity are:

- Subjective feeling (slow, fast, quiet...)
- Heart rate frequency
- Lactic acid concentration in blood

Subjective feeling

Using this parameter you merely trust your gut instinct to determine the intensity of your training. The feeling during the different training forms logically should be the following:

Recovery training and AET1 and AET2
- Comfortable
- You can still continue this tempo easily for a long time
- You breathe easily
- You can easily talk during the effort. As a matter of fact you could tell a complete story without interruptions

AET3
- Less comfortable feeling
- Tempo is not exactly easy, but nevertheless you can keep it up approximately 30 to 60 minutes
- You breathe more quickly and superficially
- Talking during running gets more difficult. Only short sentences with interruptions are still possible

Fartlek
- The feeling during this speed game depends entirely on the quality of the intensive parts
- Generally the feeling during the intensive parts is uncomfortable, and talking is difficult

Tempo interval run
- Uncomfortable feeling
- You can keep up the tempo a maximum 10 to 15 minutes
- You breathe rapidly and superficially
- Talking is almost impossible during this kind of training, and you must restrict yourself to pronouncing a few words

High intensity interval training
- Your legs and even your arms feel heavy and painful because of the piling-up of lactic acid in your muscles
- You breathe very quickly now
- Talking has become completely impossible, even for a while after finishing

This subjective feeling is an important parameter. Nevertheless you must be careful with your gut instinct. If you feel good, and you are in good shape, there is a risk that the training intensity (continuous) will be too high. Therefore it is advisable to also use other parameters to determine your optimal training intensity.

Heart rate

A commonly used method to determine the training intensity has been based on the heart rate during the effort. This parameter not only provides very important information on the intensity of your training, but also on your level of conditioning.

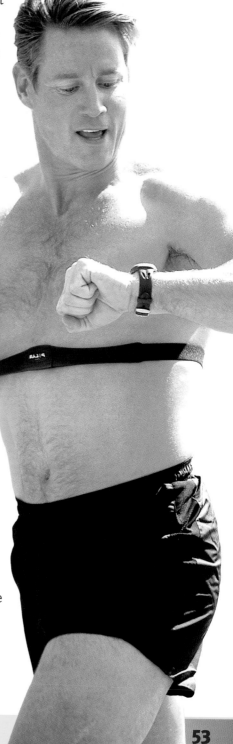

It is a fact that up to a point, the heart rate increases linearly to the increasing intensity of the training, and therefore comparing heart rates at various times gives a clear picture of the value of the training. Better conditioning translates into a lower heart rate for the same effort.

In other words, if you later notice that you can produce a higher tempo at a lower heart rate, this means that a positive training impact has taken place.
Improved conditioning is also expressed in a more rapid drop to a resting heart rate after the effort.

How can the heart rate be measured?

In the first place you can measure heart rate manually by feeling and counting the heart rate near the heart, the carotid artery or the radial artery. This method is obviously very inaccurate, especially if the heart rate is high and you cannot count immediately after the effort.

Measuring heart rates is most accurant when using a wireless heart rate monitor. Using this method, you can continuously monitor your heart rate during the effort.
Training intensity based on the percentage of the maximum heart rate.

You can determine your training intensity based on certain percentages of your maximum heart rate.

After a sound warm-up of at least ten to fifteen minutes ending with tempo accelerations, tou can determine your maximum heart rate by cycling or running for one to two minutes at full speed (for cycling preferably uphill). This maximum heart rate can be also determined during a maximum effort test at the doctor.

The maximum heart rate can be also determined by the rule of thumb "220-age". If you are 30 years old, you could conclude that your maximum heart rate is 190 beats per minute. Although this often gets close to the right number, it is best to start from your real maximum heart rate, if possible.

Remember, the maximum heart rate in itself provides absolutely no indication of your condition, and is not due to your training. The maximum heart rate will gradually decrease, however, as you get older.

The training heart rates can be inferred from the next table:

Nature of the training	% of the maximum heart frequency
Warming up/recovery training	- 70%
AET1 (Long Slow Distance)	70-75%
AET2	75-80%
AET3	80-90%
Tempo interval run	+90%
High intensity interval training	+ 94%

This method has the advantage that it is very easily determined and useful for training, but a disadvantage is the evolution of the conditioning is not taken into account at all. In other words, independent of your condition, the training heart rates will always be the same since the maximum heart rate does not change due to the influence of training.

Training intensity based on the formula of Karvonen

When calculating training intensity, the formula of Karvonen takes into account the resting heart rate, apart from the maximum heart rate.

$$\% \ (HR \ maximum - HR \ rest) + HR \ rest = HR \ during \ the \ effort$$

For example:
Your resting heart rate is 50 and your maximum heart rate is 200. You want to train to 70% of the maximum intensity. The training heart rates are then calculated as follows:

$$0.7 \ (200\text{-}50) + 50 = 155$$

Based on the formula of Karvonen you can calculate the training heart rates for the different training forms as follows:

Nature of the training	% according to Karvonen
Warm-up/recovery training	- 65%
AET1 (Long Slow Distance)	66-72%
AET2	73-76%
AET3	77-84%
Tempo interval run	85-90%
High intensity interval training	+90%

Elaborated example:

Maximum heart rate = 200
Resting heart rate = 50

- Recovery training: 0.65 (200-50) +50 = 148

- AET1 (LSD): 0.66 (200-50) +50 = 149
  0.72 (200-50) +50 = 158

- AET2: 0.73 (200-50) +50 = 159
  0.76 (200-50) +50 = 164

- AET3: 0.77 (200-50) +50 = 165
  0.84 (200-50) +50 = 176

- Tempo interval run: 0.85 (200-50) +50 = 177
  0.90 (200-50) +50 = 185

- High intensity interval: +0.90 (200-50) +50 = 185

The advantage of the formula of Karvonen is that this formula is applicable to everyone. It is also a reliable method to show a good correlation with the more specialized lactic acid tests.

An additional advantage is that by using this formula the condition of the runner is taken into account. As the resting heart rate decreases (better condition), the formula will also produce different results.

Lower limit training heart rates Long Slow Distance according to Karvonen

Hr/Hm	205	200	195	190	185	180	175	170
35	146	142	139	136	133	129	126	123
40	147	144	141	138	134	131	128	125
45	149	146	143	139	137	133	130	126
50	151	148	144	141	138	135	131	128
55	153	149	146	143	140	136	133	130
60	154	151	148	145	141	138	135	132
65	156	153	150	146	143	140	137	133
70	158	155	151	148	145	142	138	135
75	160	156	153	150	147	143	140	137
80	161	158	155	152	148	145	142	139

Upper limit training heart rates Long Slow Distance according to Karvonen

Hr/Hm	205	200	195	190	185	180	175	170
35	157	154	150	147	143	139	136	132
40	159	155	152	148	144	141	137	134
45	160	157	153	149	146	142	139	135
50	162	158	154	151	147	144	140	136
55	163	159	156	152	149	145	141	138
60	164	161	157	154	150	146	143	139
65	166	162	159	155	151	148	144	141
70	167	164	160	156	153	149	146	142
75	169	165	161	158	154	151	147	143
80	170	166	163	159	156	152	148	145

Lower limit training heart rates AET2 according to Karvonen

Hr/Hm	205	200	195	190	185	180	175	170
35	159	155	152	148	145	141	137	134
40	160	157	153	150	146	142	139	135
45	162	158	155	151	147	144	140	136
50	163	160	156	152	149	145	141	138
55	165	161	157	154	150	146	143	139
60	166	162	159	155	151	148	144	140
65	167	164	160	156	153	149	145	142
70	169	165	161	158	154	150	147	143
75	170	166	163	159	155	152	148	144
80	171	168	164	160	157	153	149	146

Upper limit training heart rates AET2 according to Karvonen

Hr/Hm	205	200	195	190	185	180	175	170
35	164	160	157	153	149	145	141	138
40	165	162	158	154	150	146	143	139
45	167	163	159	155	151	148	144	140
50	168	164	160	156	153	149	145	141
55	169	165	161	158	154	150	146	142
60	170	166	163	159	155	151	147	144
65	171	168	164	160	156	152	149	145
70	173	169	165	161	157	154	150	146
75	174	170	166	162	159	155	151	147
80	175	171	167	164	160	156	152	148

Lower limit training heart AET3 according to Karvonen

Hr/Hm	205	200	195	190	185	180	175	170
35	166	162	158	154	151	147	143	139
40	167	163	159	156	152	148	144	140
45	168	164	161	157	153	149	145	141
50	169	166	162	158	154	150	146	142
55	171	167	163	159	155	151	147	144
60	172	168	164	160	156	152	149	145
65	173	169	165	161	157	154	150	146
70	174	170	166	162	159	155	151	147
75	175	171	167	164	160	156	152	148
80	176	172	169	165	161	157	153	149

Upper limit training heart rates AET3 according to Karvonen

Hr/Hm	205	200	195	190	185	180	175	170
35	178	174	169	165	161	157	153	148
40	179	174	170	166	162	158	153	149
45	179	175	171	167	163	158	154	150
50	180	176	172	168	163	159	155	151
55	181	177	173	168	164	160	156	152
60	182	178	173	169	165	161	157	152
65	183	178	174	170	166	162	157	153
70	183	179	175	171	167	162	158	154
75	184	180	176	172	167	163	159	155
80	185	181	177	172	168	164	160	156

Lower limit training heart rates tempo interval according to Karvonen

Hr/Hm	205	200	195	190	185	180	175	170
35	180	175	171	167	163	158	154	150
40	180	176	172	168	163	159	155	151
45	181	177	173	168	164	160	156	151
50	182	178	173	169	165	161	156	152
55	183	178	174	170	166	161	157	153
60	183	179	175	171	166	162	158	154
65	184	180	176	171	167	163	159	154
70	185	181	176	172	168	164	159	155
75	186	181	177	173	169	164	160	156
80	186	182	178	174	169	165	161	157

Upper limit training heart rates tempo interval according to Karvonen

Hr/Hm	205	200	195	190	185	180	175	170
35	188	184	179	175	170	166	161	157
40	189	184	180	175	171	166	162	157
45	189	185	180	176	171	167	162	158
50	190	185	181	176	172	167	163	158
55	190	186	181	177	172	168	163	159
60	191	186	182	177	173	168	164	159
65	191	187	182	178	173	169	164	160
70	192	187	183	178	174	169	165	160
75	192	188	183	179	174	170	165	161
80	193	188	184	179	175	170	166	161

Determining the resting heart rate

It is interesting to look at measuring and interpreting the resting heart rate. It's best to measure your resting heart rate lying down, just after awakening. The circumstances for measuring resting heart rate must always be the same.

What can you infer from this?

The resting heart rate gives you an insight into the evolution of your shape.
It is common practice that if your shape improves, your resting heart rate decreases. On the other hand, if you train no longer or less often, after a while your resting heart rate will increase.

Your resting heart rate can be considered the barometer of the body.

An elevated resting heart rate can be a sign:

- That you have insufficiently recovered from the efforts made, either in a training session, or during a race.

  If you are well trained, an increase of only a few heart beats (about 5) or 10% obliges you to be careful.

  If you are less well trained, your resting heart rate is more affected by previous training labor. In this case your resting heart rate can be 7 to 10 beats or 15-20% higher before an alarm bell will sound.

  If your resting heart rate is raised, you should insert a rest day or a lighter training session. Continuous attention to the resting heart rate remains necessary.

- Of a viral infection such as influenza, before other symptoms appear.

  Less training, or even complete rest, are required to prevent reducing the resistance of your body further against the rising infection. Recovery will be much quicker than if you continue to train, risking a more serious infection and extended illness.

  A regular and precise measurement and interpretation of the morning pulse curve can spare you a lot of trouble.

Notes

A low resting heart rate is not an absolute measure of your conditioning. A runner having 45 for resting heart rate is not necessarily in better condition than an athlete having a resting heart rate of 50. Moreover, a low resting heart rate does not always guarantee that your form is optimum (see below).

Factors influencing the heart rate

If you use the heart rate monitor to determine your training intensity, you should take into account a number of factors, apart from training intensity, that may influence the heart rate.

Illness
If you are ill, you have a (much) higher heart rate than usual, both during rest and during effort. It cannot be stressed too often that training when you are sick is useless and even dangerous. A sick body is not trainable.

Loss of fluids
Loss of fluids increases the heart rate during effort. It is thus very important to drink sufficiently during all training sessions and races.

Altitude
When you go on an altitude-training period, you will see that your heart rate at rest and during efforts is higher than usual.
After an acclimatization period of a few days, the heart rateat rest drops to the normal value. This also is the indicator that training can now be resumed as usual.
However, it is much more difficult to attain the normal maximum heart rate during altitude training.

Medicines
Some medicines have a direct impact on the heart rate.

Nutrition
Eating food full of carbohydrates before training, and drinking energy drinks during training sessions and races, leads to a lower heart rate.
Someone who neglects to replace his carbohydrate stores after high intensity training sessions and races will no longer be able to obtain a high heart rate after a while. This will lead to being overtrained.

A drop in temperature
A drop in temperature during a long-term effort brings along a drop in heart rate.

Stress

During a race, the heart rate is higher than usual, especially for runners under stress. For these athletes, it is not very useful to wear a heart rate monitor during races, and does not make sense to measure the resting heart rate on the morning of a race.

The muscle mass used

Using more muscle mass during the effort increases the heart rate. That is why it is easier to attain a higher heart rate when cycling uphill than when cycling on a flat track.

Temperature and humidity

The heart rate increases in warm weather and high humidity, both in rest and during efforts. The heart rate reaches its most normal values between 16°C/60°F and 20° C/68°F. If the temperature is lower than 16°C/60°F, it gets more difficult to reach the heart rate limits for the different types of training. Starting at 12°C/54°F, the heart rate limits can be reduced by one heart rate per degree.

Overtraining

An athlete who is over-trained can no longer reach their maximum heart rate. The heart rate during effort is thus lower than usual, And is sometimes wrongfully interpreted as a positive sign (a lower heart rate for the same effort).

CONCLUSION

The heart rate monitor is a very useful instrument to control your training intensity. You must take into account, however, the different factors that can influence your heart rate. The heart rate monitor is most efficient for a runner during training segments where you train to a relatively low heart rate.

Lactic acid concentration in blood

A more scientific method to determine your training intensity is determining the lactic acid concentration in your blood during an effort.

At rest, the lactic acid concentration in the blood amounts to 1 to 2 mmol/liter. This lactic acid concentration remains constant as long as the athlete remains at rest or trains at a moderate intensity. As long as the lactic acid concentration remains stable or only increases slightly, the effort can be continued for a very long time, theoretically speaking, because the lactic acid formed is also being removed during the effort.

As the effort intensity continues to increase, the amoung of lactic acid also starts to increase. As the intensity continues to increase, the lactic acid concentration rises more dramatically, and at high intensity will eventually show a very strong increase curve. At this moment you will be obliged to stop the effort or to strongly scale back the intensity. For a well-trained athlete, the running speed will be higher before the curve shows a strong increase than for a less well-trained athlete.

Laboratory test

This is generally tested using a graduated effort test on a running treadmill. This means that the speed is being raised (depending on the test protocol) after a few minutes. The time span of one effort stage should take at least 4 minutes to allow a constant lactic acid value to be reached.

The training recommendation is based on the course of the lactic acid curve. The point where the lactic acid curve shows a strong increase (heart rate 164) is vital. We can conclude that the threshold is situated here.

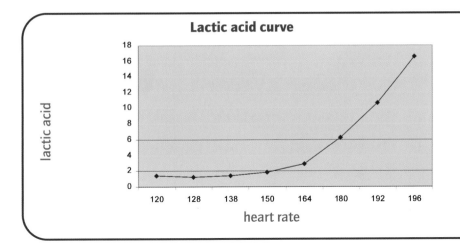

Field test

In addition to the laboratory test, a so-called field test is used as well. The test is carried out on an athletic track, where you do a stipulated distance, for example 2000 meters, three to four times, and each time at a higher speed. After each separate distance, the time, heart rate and lactic acid concentration in the blood are determined. Afterwards these parameters are compared in a graph.

The advantage of this field test is that it is more specific, meaning the real running situation is approximated more closely than in a laboratory test. The disadvantage is, however, that it is extremely difficult to standardize the test circumstances (temperature, wind, surface), so comparisons between several tests are less reliable.

CHAPTER 6

Good to know

The output of your training

If you start training as a beginner or after a period of inactivity, you will see your condition improve quickly. You can soon cope with a larger training volume, and your running speed also increases steadily.

It is, unfortunately, not the case that more and more training brings along a linearly proportional increase in your performance capacity. It is impossible to constantly keep making the same kind of progress. Over time the increase in training impact diminishes, even despite a rising training load. Eventually, it gets very difficult, almost impossible, to still make progress. You run a 'best time' once, and even giving it all you can you cannot repeat that performance. You have reached your peak.

This means the better your condition is, the more difficult it is to still make progress. This is called the principle of the reduced added value.

This observation often is discouraging. If you are very ambitious you will not easily admit that you cannot make any further progress. The risk of overtraining is at its highest at that moment. By still forcing up training, you can exceed your capacity.

Alternative training

To achieve top performances, you must train hard but responsibly. It is also important that you mostly train within your own sport branch. Specifically, a cyclist strains the same organic systems as a long distance runner during his specific training, and he has an equally excellent aerobic endurance capacity, but he won't be able to achieve a decent running performance. The training transfer of one sport branch to the other is very limited. Cardiovascular, muscle and nerve systems of the body react specifically to the particular demands made on them.

The main reasons why cycling training can't improve running performance and vice-versa are:

- the use of different muscle groups during the specific movement
- the difference in mechanical strain on the muscle groups during the specific movement
- the difference in muscle labor during the specific movement

Nevertheless, it can still be sometimes useful to integrate other training forms along with specific run training in your program.

You can then, aside from your normal running program, take refuge in alternative, less straining training forms, like cycling, aquajogging and strength training. These alternative training sessions can be also be very useful to maintain your conditioning level if you are not able to run due to a overload injury.

Cycling

Cycling is an excellent means to maintain your general endurance capacity when you cannot run for whatever reason, or when you consider additional training to be necessary. To obtain the same training impact you must train at least twice as long.

TIP:

Take into account that your training heart rates for cycling training is 10 to 20 beats lower than for running training.

Aquajogging

Aquajogging means jogging in deep water. You have a belt around your chest, so you hang "vertically" in the water. You then start doing running movements. You can support this movement easily using your arms..

Aquajogging is a perfect alternative training form which comes very close to running, and can be carried out even if recovering from almost every possible injury. A period of running inactivity can be perfectly covered by means of aquajogging, without much condition loss. You can do essentially the same kind of training as your ordinary running program. It is, however, difficult to reach the same training heart rates while aquajogging as you do during normal running training.

Example of tempo interval training by means of aquajogging:
- 15 minutes warming up
- 6 times 4 minutes high tempo with good support of the arms (equivalent to 6 times 1000 meters on the track), recovery – 1 to 2 minutes quiet
- 15 minutes cooling down.

Strength training

The question whether strength training is useful for a long distance runner is very controversial. On the one hand, more strength can lead to greater length of steps, and you can use it when running uphill. On the other hand strength training can also lead to weight increase, which is noxious for long distance running performances.

In any case, strength training for a long distance runner must meet the following conditions:

- only the leg muscles must be trained. Training of the muscles of the torso and upper arms is of little significance, with the exception of the abdominal muscles. Strong abs can ensure a good pelvis consolidation and help avoid lower back complaints.

- to obtain training impact, you must train 2 times per week with a break of 2 days.

- you must train with light weights, doing many repetitions. The training weight is 40 to 50% of the maximum weight that can be moved one time over the whole movement cycle of the exercise.

A training advancement for 8 weeks can look as follows:

Week	Repetitions	Series
1	10	3
2	12	3
3	10	4
4	12	4
5	10	5
6	12	5
7	15	5
8	17	5
9	20	5

Between each series you have a restricted recovery time from 30 s to 1 minute.

TIP:

Avoid strain on the knee joint during strength training. Bend the knees when squatting (bending the legs with a weight on the shoulders) no deeper than 90°. Limit training the hamstrings to avoid shortening these muscles.

Interrupt your running program

Reaching your individual maximum performance level demands a long-term and well-reasoned progressive training program. Interrupting your training, because of illness or injury, quickly causes a contrary impact: in a very short time, hard-earned conditioning can be almost completely lost. It takes much less time to lose your conditioning that it did to build it. This principle especially applies in those sports in which the muscles use lots of oxygen, like long distance running.

Research has nevertheless proven that you can preserve a certain performance level during some 20 weeks when training labor is scaled back 40 % during this period. But you can only achieve this if the same training intensity is maintained. Your condition does not disappear if you train slightly less for some weeks.

It is also true that the time needed to reach a former level of conditioning after a training stop is significantly shorter than the time initially needed to reach this level. Although specific training has by far the highest output value, in case of injury it is best to keep your general condition on a good level by means of alternative training.

CHAPTER 7

Plan your training

During the year you should vary your training – both in type and intensity. A training year is divided into a number of periods, and the training sessions and races must be planned to help you reach specific goals during these different periods.
This training planning can be spread out over:

several years: long-range plan
- 1 year: macro-cycle or year planning
- 4-8 weeks: meso-cycle
- 1-3 weeks: micro-cycle

Year planning

Generally speaking a year planning is subdivided into
- a preparation period
- a specific period
- a race period
- a relative recovery period

If your year consists of 2 race periods the above-mentioned periods will occur twice a year.

The preparation period:

At the beginning of the preparation period you must not only be physically, but also mentally reloaded to start a new training program. A thorough medical check-up is essential.

The objectives for the next race season are fixed, and will to a great extent determine the rhythm of the training set-up. Roughly speaking, you plan during this period a gradual advancement from quiet (extensive) training sessions to more intensive training sessions. The intensive training sessions increase as the race season approaches.

Nevertheless you can do some more intensive training sessions rather early in the preparation period to stimulate the anaerobic capacity.

The advantages of this approach are:
- You strain the different energy supply systems. The variation in training ensures that both the fat metabolism and the carbohydrate metabolism are stimulated.
- There is a positive influence on the capacity for oxygen intake. The maximum oxygen intake capacity is not only improved by slow duration training sessions, but also by training sessions involving the aerobic-anaerobic area.
- You avoid monotony, thereby reducing the risk of overtraining.
- You have less chance of stagnation in the performance level. Performance improvement is only possible when you train in a varied way.

Nevertheless the training volume during this period generally is more important than the intensity of the training sessions. In the beginning of the preparation period you must pay close attention to the development of aerobic endurance. Therefore the long, easy endurance training sessions remain by far the most important type of training.

This does not mean that these training sessions must be monotonous. For instance, at the beginning of a Long Slow Distance, after the warming-up phase, you can do some short, submaximal rhythm changes.

The specific period:

During the previous period the foundation was laid for race-specific training sessions. The training volume is now scaled back and the training intensity strongly increases. Because training sessions at higher intensity can soon have a negative influence on the basic endurance capacity, you must make sure that you still take the easy aerobic endurance workouts sufficiently into consideration in the total training volume.

During this period you can, as part of your training, run some shorter races to acquire race rhythm and to get a good insight into your possible shortcomings.

TIP:

The intensification of the training also means that you must pay proper attention to the recovery phase.

The race period:

This is a very difficult period because you must find a balance between races, recovery, specific race training and basic training. Lacking the latter makes it very difficult to keep a peak condition for a long time. Therefore it is necessary to regularly plan a race stop so you can spend sufficient time on recovery and basic training

The relative recovery period:

After a race period you are tired, both mentally and physically. One to two weeks complete training stop is generally enough. After this training stop you can resume exercising through sports, preferably by means of alternative activities such as swimming, cycling, playing tennis etc. The aim for this period is not raising the specific performance possibilities, but maintaining a certain fitness level as a basis for the coming preparation period.
The relative recovery period generally lasts four to six weeks.

The mesocycles

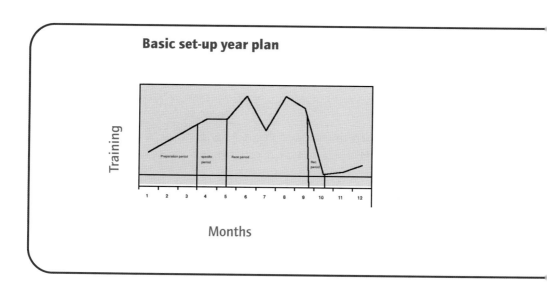

Basic set-up year plan

After you have planned your training roughly for the whole year, you must plan further, in periods of four to eight weeks. These periods are called mesocycles.

The standard cycle

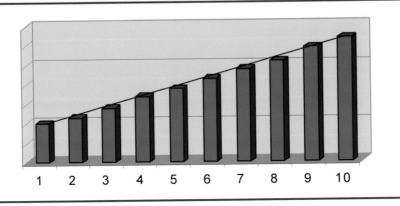

In this cycle you have a gradual and progressive increase of the training volume. To prevent overload this increase in training volume cannot exceed 15% per week. It is an excellent cycle for the preparation period, especially for forcing up the training quantity. The disadvantage of this cycle is the fact that no recovery periods are planned. Therefore there is a risk of overload.

The increasing block-system cycle

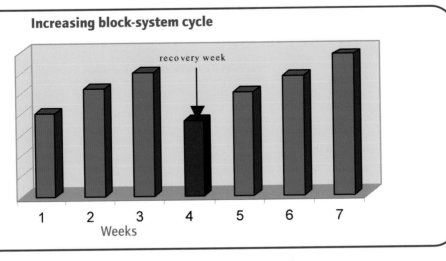

Increasing block-system cycle

recovery week

Weeks

The increase of the training volume occurs in a wave-like movement. After three weeks a recovery week is integrated, after which the training volume increases more strongly than during the first three weeks. This is an excellent set-up to keep the risk of overload injuries low.

The decreasing block-system cycle

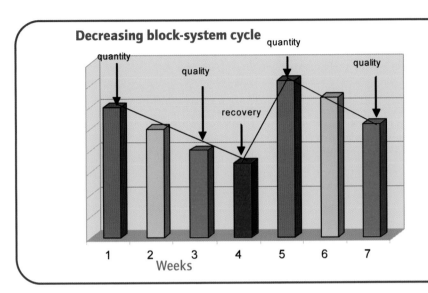

Here, too, the training set-up occurs in a wave-like movement. This cycle is suitable for forcing up training quality: if the volume decreases the training intensity can increase. The decreasing block-system cycle is used especially during the specific period.

Due to the great transition between week four and five, there is a risk of overload in the fifth week.

The thrust cycle

Training alternates between high and low strain. Due to the great difference in volume between weeks there is a risk on overload. This cycle is especially suitable for the race period (peaks).

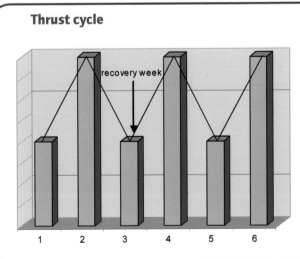

The microcycle

In a week cycle as well a wave-like motion should be observed in the intensity.

You would rather not train intensively two days in a row.
An intensive training day is followed by a training day in which you train to a more moderate intensity. Afterwards a relatively light training day follows.

One day per week is preferably reserved as recovery day. If you are well trained this generally means a relative recovery day on which you train very quietly (one training session). If you are in less good shape you best opt for a recovery day on which you do not train at all.

It is important to plan your training sessions by starting with the long-term view, then developing the plan more and more for the short term. You must know in advance where you want to end up for the year.

Nevertheless the plan should always show enough flexibility. There are always factors, such as weather conditions, illness, fatigue etc. that will disturb that planning. This means that planning cannot be entirely fixed, but that it will continuously have to be adjusted.

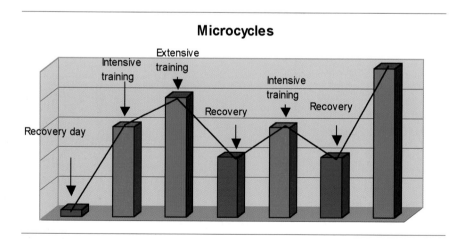

CHAPTER 8

12 week plan for a half-marathon

After you have finished your 9-week program for 10 kilometers, you are able to face the next challenge: to reach the finish of a half-marathon (21 km).

Still, the best you can do is to adjust your body to the increased running load and therefore run for a couple of months maximum two up to two and a half hours a week. Having done this you can start with the proper preparation of the 21 kilometers.

The half marathon is a very atractive distance, because it already appeals to your imagination, but does not yet demand too much of your body.

Four training sessions per week should be enough, and your longest training session should certainly never last longer than 90 minutes. All this can still be easily incorporated in your normal work rhythm. In addition, the risk of overload injuries still remains rather limited.

With the following 12-week training schedule you should be able to succeed in your new objective.

Week 1

It should not be your intention to suddenly and drastically force up your training volume and your training intensity. During this first week of your actual preparation for a half-marathon, you elaborate on the base program for the 10 kilometers. The running intensity mostly remains still relatively low. Only during one training session should you run to higher intensity.

Day	Training	Intensity description
Monday	Recovery day	
Tuesday	35 min easy running	Level AET2
Wednesday		
Thursday	60 min easy running	Level AET1
Friday		
Saturday	10 min warm-up 3 x 10 min higher tempo, rec. 3 min slowing down 10 min cool down	Level AET3
Sunday	40 min very easy running	Level AET1
TOTAL	**191 minutes**	

Week 2

The total running volume increases, but to avoid overload injuries this increase is still very limited, between 10 and 15 percent. There also is an increase in the intensity of training. But the heart rate during these more intensive training sessions does not exceed the level of AET3.

Day	Training	Intensity description
Monday	Recovery day	
Tuesday	10 min warm up 5 x 5 min higher tempo, rec. 3 min slowing down 10 min cool down	Level AET3
Wednesday		
Thursday	65 min easy running	Level AET1
Friday		
Saturday	15 min warm up 20 min higher tempo 15 min cool down	Level AET3
Sunday	45 min very easy running	Level AET1
TOTAL	**217 minutes**	

Week 3

As was mentioned during the previous chapter, you will want to work according to the increasing block-system cycle. This means that during this third week you still increase the total running volume and the running intensity, just before you insert a recovery week. But obey your body in any case. If you feel tired, you can always replace the more intensive training of Saturday with easier training.

Day	Training	Intensity description
Monday	Recovery day	
Tuesday	10 min warm up 40 min fartlek, with short, more intensive parts 10 min cool down	Till maximum level tempo interval training (limited)
Wednesday		
Thursday	70 min easy run	Level AET1
Friday		
Saturday	10 min warm up 25 min higher tempo 10 min cool down	Level AET3
Sunday	50 min easy run	Level AET1
TOTAL	**225 minutes**	

Week 4

This week is a recovery week. Once you get the hang of it, you are inclined to always want to run more. You must keep in mind that training only pays off when it is followed by a recovery period. This does not mean that training must be interrupted entirely, but that both the total training volume and the training intensity are significantly scaled back.

Day	Training	Intensity description
Monday	Recovery day	
Tuesday	30 min jogging	Level recovery training
Wednesday		
Thursday	40 min very easy run	Level AET1
Friday		
Saturday	10 min warm up 15 min higher tempo 10 min cool down	Level AET3
Sunday	30 min jogging	Level recovery training
TOTAL	**135 minutes**	

Week 5

During the past relative recovery week, all previous training was able to produce full impact on your body. You have undoubtedly reached a higher conditioning level, and you will be feeling fit to restart a new three week advancement. During this week the total training volume is somewhat higher than during week 1.

Day	Training	Intensity description
Monday	Recovery day	
Tuesday	45 min easy running	Level AET2
Wednesday		
Thursday	60 min easy running	Level AET1
Friday		
Saturday	10 min warm up 4 x 8 min higher tempo, rec. 2 min slowing down 10 min cool down	Level AET3
Sunday	40 min very easy running	Level AET1
TOTAL	**203 minutes**	

Week 6

During this week (on Tuesday) you do a new type of training, namely a pyramid run. This means that you run a certain duration at a higher tempo, followed by the same duration running easily. The duration is subsequently forced up a couple of times (quickly and slowly carried out), whereupon you scale back in the reverse direction.

Day	Training	Intensity description
Monday	Recovery day	
Tuesday	10 min warming up 1 min – 2min – 3min – 3min – 2min – 1min pyramid run. 10 min cooling down	Level AET3
Wednesday		
Thursday	70 min easy running	Level AET1
Friday		
Saturday	15 min warm up 25 min higher tempo 15 min cool down	Level AET3
Sunday	50 min very easy running	Level AET1
TOTAL	**218 minutes**	

Week 7

At the end of this week you will reach a total of more than four hours of run training. This is the highest weekly volume so far. The risk of overload injuries is very real considering this quantity of training. Therefore emphasis is put on a very easy running pace, and only very limited training at a higher tempo has been inserted in this week's program.

Day	Training	Intensity description
Monday	Recovery day	
Tuesday	75 min easy running	Level AET1
Wednesday		
Thursday	60 min easy running After 10 min warm up 4 times an acceleration of approximately 10 s, followed by 1 min jogging. Rest of the training – easy running	Level AET2
Friday		
Saturday	80 min easy running	Level AET1
Sunday	40 min easy running	Level AET2
TOTAL	**255 minutes**	

Week 8

After an advancement of three weeks you will reach a point to scale back training significantly. Like in week four the emphasis is on less training volume and intensity. This relative recovery week will enable you to start the last phase of the half-marathon scheme having fresh legs.

Day	Training	Intensity description
Monday	Recovery day	
Tuesday	30 min jogging	Level recovery training
Wednesday		
Thursday	50 min easy running	Level AET1
Friday		
Saturday	10 min warm up 20 min higher tempo 10 min cool down	Level AET3
Sunday	30 min jogging	Level recovery training
TOTAL	**150 minutes**	

Week 9

During this week training is again forced up to a level higher than during the fifth week. Pyramid running is planned again. The tempo during the faster parts of this training must feel uncomfortable, but you must ensure that you are able to run just as fast at the end of this pyramid running as at the beginning.

Day	Training	Intensity description
Monday	Recovery day	
Tuesday	10 min warm up 1 min – 2 min – 3 min – 4 min – 3 min – 2 min – 1 min pyramid running. 10 min cool down	Level tempo interval training
Wednesday		
Thursday	70 min easy running	Level AET1
Friday		
Saturday	15 min warm up 30 min higher tempo 15 min cool down	Level AET3
Sunday	40 min easy running	Level AET1
TOTAL	**221 minutes**	

Week 10

The half-marathon is now no longer far off. You should now be more or less ready to complete this running distance without too many problems. That is why you should be able to run 90 minutes continuously for the first time this week. It is best to do this training with someone of the same level. The tempo must be such that you can always keep talking.

Day	Training	Intensity description
Monday	Recovery day	
Tuesday	60 min easy running, after 10 min 6 x 4 min higher tempo, rec. 2 min jogging	Level AET2, during more intensive parts till level AET3
Wednesday		
Thursday	70 min easy running, between 50 and 60 min higher tempo. Last 10 min slowing down	Level AET1 Intensive part until level tempo-interval.
Friday		
Saturday	90 min easy running	Level AET1
Sunday	30 min jogging	Recovery
TOTAL	**250 minutes**	

Week 11

During this next to last week, extra attention will be once more be paid to the total volume. Your endurance capacity will then reach the level you need to be able to run 21 kilometers one week later. Since you also have to pay attention to a faster running pace, this is a very high-charged week. You should not be reluctant to scale back training if you start feeling too tired.

Day	Training	Intensity description
Monday	Recovery day	
Tuesday	70 min easy running, between 20 and 30 min, and between 50 and 60 min each time higher tempo.	Level AET2, during more intensive parts till level AET3
Wednesday		
Thursday	70 min easy running	Level AET1
Friday		
Saturday	90 min easy running Followed after 10 min 6 x 15 s climax running (accelerate towards the end), rec. each time by 1 min jogging. Afterwards ongoing easy running	Level AET1
Sunday	30 min jogging	Level recovery training
TOTAL	**260 minutes**	

Week 12

You have completed a firm training advancement, and you are undoubtedly ready for your task. During this last week it is particularly important to let the past training have its impact. It really does not make any sense to start working extra hard while training. You should certainly pay attention to enough rest. Training is thus strongly scaled back, so that you can appear extremely fit at the start of the half-marathon.

Day	Training	Intensity description
Monday	Recovery day	
Tuesday	30 min jogging	Level recovery training
Wednesday		
Thursday	45 min easy running Instinctively still some tempo alternations	Level AET1, to maximum level AET3
Friday		
Saturday	30 min jogging	Level recovery training
Sunday	**Half-marathon**	

CHAPTER 9

12 week plan for a marathon

Completing a marathon is the ultimate dream of a lot of joggers. Everyone knows someone among their acquaintances who has succeeded in a marathon. This means it is not an impossible task, but it remains a task which demands the necessary preparation.

Finishing a marathon

In the marathon of New York, probably the biggest and most famous marathon of the world, more than half of its participants need more than 4 hours to get to the finish line. Thousands of runners even finish after more than 5 hours of running. However, this doesn't diminish their joy and satisfaction! On the contrary: every one who finishes a marathon is a winner!

A finishing time of 4 up to 5 hours and even longer in a marathon seems slow, certainly in comparison with the top times now being obtained. But make no mistake, the long duration in particular will start to bother you after a while: repeated, long-term contact with the hard surface will place a tough burden on the muscles, tendons and joints. The resulting pain is made worse over time due to the exhaustion of the energy supplies in the muscles, particularly if the tempo is somewhat too high.

A runner, for example, who runs faster than 2 hours and 30 minutes, produces another type of challenge. From the start he runs against the limit of his capacity much more so than the 4 hour runner. That makes his race especially tough.

It is best to plan your first marathon in the fall, in September or October. You will not need to do the most important preparation during the cold and dark winter months, and you can fully enjoy pleasant temperatures and the longer light of day in the planning of your training sessions. This is important if you have to combine your preparation with a normal day job, like most people.

Moreover, you can quietly recover afterwards for a number of weeks. It is better to have your recovery period in the winter than in the summer.

Of course you can plan some other races during the summer months, such as some street races over a relatively short distance (10 to 15 kilometers). During the direct preparation period it is advisable to run half-marathon. You'll run this race at a higher tempo than your marathon tempo, so you get used to the running rhythm. You can also test your fluid and energy supply.

To finish a marathon, regardless of the finishing time, it's necessary to be able to run for at least six months at a distance of an average 40 to 50 kilometers a week at a steady pace. It's really not necessary to run at a high speed or practice interval training.

   During the last couple of weeks before a marathon you should run once a week for 20 to 25 kilometers with a low intensity, level AET1. It's advisable to do this long run on a hard surface.

A top week during the last six weeks can be as follows:

Day/Dag	training	Intensity
Monday	Day off	
Tuesday	2 km very easy running	Level AET1
	8 km higher pace	Level AET2
	2 km very easy running	Level AET1
	Total: 12 km	
Wednesday	5 km jog	Level recovery
Thursday		
Friday	10 km easy running (10 km)	Level AET1
Saturday		
Sunday	20 – 25 km easy running	Level AET1
TOTAL	**Approximately 50 km**	

A marathon in 4 hours

If you want to complete a marathon in approximately 4 hours, meaning at a tempo of 10.5 kilometers per hour (5 min 42s for each kilometer), you need a preparation of approximately one year.

This is required because you cannot throw yourself just like that into the marathon adventure. You must be capable of processing a training volume of 50 to 60 kilometers during a number of weeks. The risk of injuries must be kept as tiny as possible, but this can only be done by means of a sufficiently long and progressive training advancement! Normally you also need to be able to run 10 kilometers in less than 48 minutes. With a training volume of 50 to 60 kilometers per week this should not cause any problems.

To finish a marathon in 4 hours, it is not really necessary to do fast tempo training sessions. You should work particularly for the advancement of a very broad, aerobic endurance base. This means that the aerobic training sessions, especially the Long Slow Distance training sessions, take a very important, almost exclusive place in your training program.

One to two times per week you can move the tempo slightly higher. But restrict yourself even then to the AET3 level.

Concerning the longest run in preparation for the marathon, there are quite a lot of different opinions. Some advise that you do aerobic runs of 30 to 35 kilometers in length. The mental aspect of preparation would be especially important here. If you can finish these distances without too many problems during training, you will get more confidence to succeed for the full 42 kilometers as well. Other people think that such training distances are too long for runners who only do 50 to 60 kilometers per week, and have a demolishing rather than constructive impact. For top runners, who run 200 kilometers/week and more, this 30 kilometer running distance no problem!

TIP:

You may regularly interrupt your longest aerobic runs, certainly in the beginning, with some walking minutes.

The last 12 weeks before the race

Prior to starting these last 12 weeks of training you must be able to finish 45 kilometers per week spread out over 4 to 5 training sessions without any problems. Then you are ready to prepare yourself to your first marathon over a period of three months.

The aim is to complete the race within 4 hours without having to walk. This advancement occurs thanks to the increasing block-system cycle (see diagram below).

TIP:

Do one of your aerobic runs on a hard surface each week. The rest of the training sessions you preferably can do on a soft surface.

Week 1

To start your 12-week plan for a marathon in less than 4 hours with a good chance of success, you must be able to run at least 45 kilometers during the first week. You should mostly run at low tempo. This is necessary to build a broad endurance base. You should run the faster parts at a speed which is higher than the tempo you want to run during the marathon. If your objective is four hours, you run these more intensive parts to a speed higher than 5:42/kilometer.

Day	Training	Intensity description
Monday	Recovery day	
Tuesday	15 min running easily 3 x 6 min faster than running pace marathon, rec. 5 min running easily 15 min running easily (10 km)	Level AET3
Wednesday	35 min jogging (5-6 km)	Level recovery training
Thursday	60 min easy running	Level AET1
Friday		
Saturday	90 min easy running (15 km)	Level AET1
Sunday	35 min jogging (5-6 km)	Level recovery training
TOTAL	**275 minutes** **(approximately 45 kilometers)**	

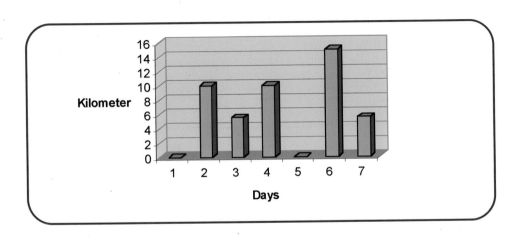

Week 2

During the second week you follow the same pattern as during the first week. The training is progressively forced up, but you keep putting emphasis on training volume, rather than on training intensity. Less than ten per cent of your total training time is spent training at a tempo higher than your planned marathon training tempo.

Day	Training	Intensity description
Monday	Recovery day	
Tuesday	15 min running easily	Level AET3
	4 x 6 min faster than running pace marathon, rec. 5 min running easily	
	15 min easy running	Level AET2
	(11 – 12 km)	
Wednesday	35 min jogging (5-6 km)	Level recovery training
Thursday	65 min easy running (10-11 km)	Level AET1
Friday	recovery day	
Saturday	100 min easy running (17-18 km)	Level AET1
Sunday	30 min jogging (5 km)	Level recovery training

TOTAL	304 minutes (approximately 50 kilometers)

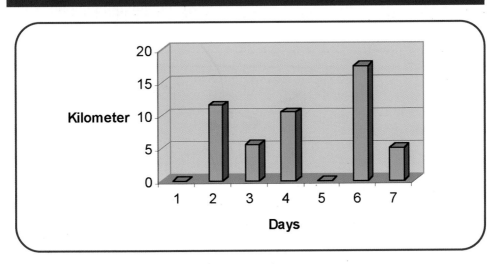

Week 3

Since the advancement follows the increasing block-system cycle, this is the last week of advancement before a recovery week is inserted. The proportion of the more intensive training sessions with respect to the aerobic training sessions remains the same as during last week. Do not be tempted to higher running pace, even if you feel good!

Day	Training	Intensity description
Monday	Recovery day	
Tuesday	15 min running easily	Level AET3
	3 x 10 min faster than running pace marathon, rec. 5 min running easily	
	20 min easy running	Level AET2
	(12-13 km)	
Wednesday	35 min jogging (5-6 km)	Level recovery training
Thursday	75 min easy running (12-13 km)	Level AET1
Friday	Recovery day	
Saturday	110 min easy running (18-19 km)	Level AET1
Sunday	30 min jogging (5 km)	Level recovery training

TOTAL	325 minutes (approximately 55 kilometers)

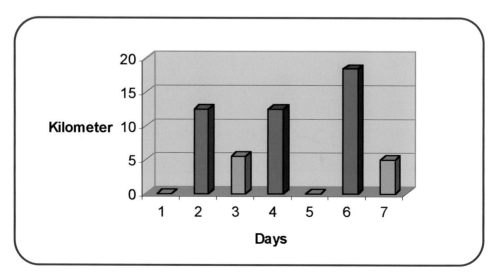

Week 4

During the fourth week training is drastically scaled back. This is necessary to get the maximal value from the training you've done the previous three weeks. You should not worry about skipping a couple of days running this week. On the days you do run, the pace remains very low.

Day	Training	Intensity description
Monday		
Tuesday	30 min jogging (5 km)	Level recovery training
Wednesday		
Thursday	45 min easy running (7-8 km)	Level AET1
Friday		
Saturday	90 min easy running (15 km)	Level AET1
Sunday	30 min jogging (5-6 km)	Level recovery training
TOTAL	**195 minutes (approximately 33 kilometers)**	

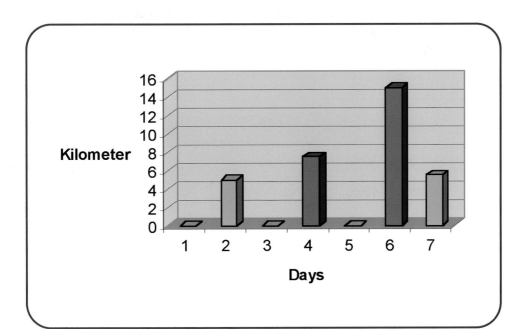

Week 5

You take up training again, following the pattern of the three first weeks of the training advancement. This means that the emphasis still is on relatively easy training sessions, and that once during this week you run to a tempo which is higher than the tempo you've planned for your race. Make sure the tempo during the longest aerobic run remains low. You should be able to talk during this training session.

Day	Training	Intensity description
Monday	Recovery day	
Tuesday	10 min running easily 5 x 6 min faster than running pace marathon, rec. 5 min running easily 10 min cooling down (11 – 12 km)	Level AET3
Wednesday	35 min jogging (5-6 km)	Level recovery training
Thursday	65 min easy running (10-11 km)	Level AET2
Friday	Recovery day	
Saturday	100 min easy running (17-18 km)	Level AET1
Sunday	30 min jogging (5 – 6 km)	Level recovery training
TOTAL	**300 minutes** **(approximately 50 kilometers)**	

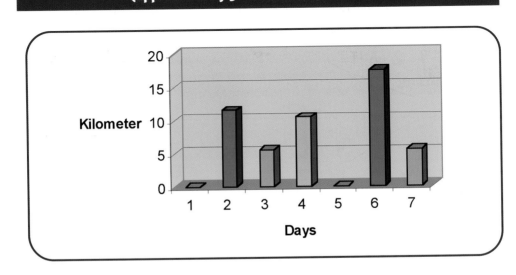

Week 6

At the end of this week, a race over half the distance is planned. This is not a target race for you, but is a means to acquire a certain race rhythm and to test your fluid intake (thirst quencher and energy drinks). Try to run a little bit faster than your target racetempo, which means at least faster than 5:42/kilometer! Make sure you don't get carried away by the enthusiasm of the other runners. Under all circumstances, try to keep your own running pace which you have determined in advance.

Because this is not a target race for you, training is not really scaled back during the preparation for this race. Only during the last 2 days should you train very restrictively.

Day	Training	Intensity description
Monday	15 min running easily 2 x 8 min faster than running pace marathon, rec. 5 min running easily 15 min running easily (10-11 km)	Level AET3 Level AET2
Tuesday	30 min jogging (5-6 km)	Level recovery training
Wednesday	Recovery day	
Thursday	85 min easy running (13-14 km)	Level AET1
Friday	Recovery day	
Saturday	30 min running easily (5 km)	Level recovery training
Sunday	Race 21 km	

TOTAL	315 minutes (approximately 55 kilometers)

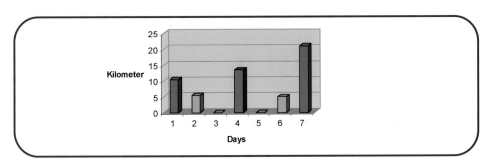

Week 7

The Sunday race probably demanded a lot of you. The first days of this week are thus dominated by the necessary recovery. Two days of rest and/or very limited training are required, followed by resuming normal training with a very easy aerobic run. The total training volume now approaches sixty kilometers per week.

Day	Training	Intensity description
Monday	Recovery day	
Tuesday	35 min jogging (5-6 km)	Level recovery training
Wednesday	80 min easy running (13-14 km)	Level AET2
Thursday	Recovery day	
Friday	15 min running easily 3 x 10 min faster than running pace marathon, rec. 5 min running easily	Level AET3
	20 min easy running (12-13 km)	Level AET2
Saturday	35 min jogging (5-6 km)	Level recovery training
Sunday	110 min easy running (18-19 km)	Level AET1

TOTAL	340 minutes (approximately 57 kilometers)

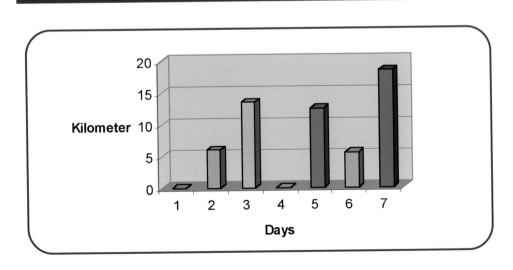

Week 8

After three weeks of increasing strain it is time to let your body recover and let the past efforts produce maximum output. You best restrict yourself to very easy and relatively short running training sessions. Towards the end of the week you do one longer training session (90 min), to help keep your basic endurance on a good level.

Day	Training	Intensity description
Monday	Recovery day	
Tuesday	35 min jogging (5-6 km)	Level recovery training
Wednesday	Recovery day	
Thursday	50 min easy running (8-9 km)	Level AET1
Friday	Recovery day	
Saturday	90 min very easy running (15 km)	Level AET1
Sunday	35 min jogging (5-6 km)	Level recovery training
TOTAL	**210 minutes** **(approximately 35 kilometers)**	

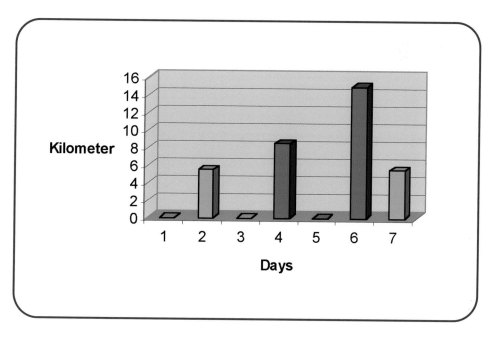

Week 9

The last phase of the preparation for your marathon has started. Now you must pay attention to implementing very long aerobic training sessions. Thus, during the following three weeks, an aerobic run of more than 2 hours is inserted in the training program. The tempo during these aerobic training sessions must consciously be kept very slow, to stimulate maximum fat oxidation.

Day	Training	Intensity description
Monday	Recovery day	
Tuesday	15 min running easily 2 x 15 min faster than running pace marathon, rec. 5 min running easily	Level AET3
	20 min easy running (11 – 12 km)	Level AET2
Wednesday	30 min jogging (5 km)	Level recovery training
Thursday	90 min easy running (15 km)	Level AET2
Friday	Recovery day	
Saturday	130 min easy running (21-22 km)	Level AET1
Sunday	30 min jogging (5 km)	Level recovery training

TOTAL	**350 minutes (approximately 60 kilometers)**

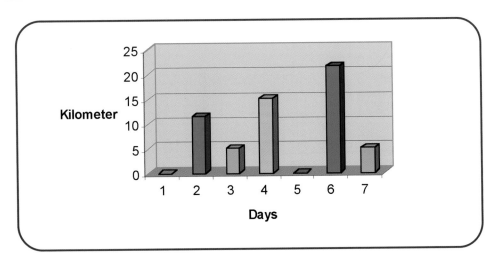

Week 10

At the end of this week there is an important test. Try to run 25 km faster than 2 hours and 15 min. – this means faster than 5:30/kilometer. You should succeed in this test rather easily if you want to finish the marathon in two weeks in less than 4 hours.

Day	Training	Intensity description
Monday	Recovery day	
Tuesday	20 min running easily	
	35 min faster than running pace marathon	Level AET3
	20 min easy running (13-14 km)	Level AET2
Wednesday	35 min jogging (5 km)	Level recovery training
Thursday	100 min easy running (17 km)	Level AET1
Friday	Recovery day	
Saturday	30 min jogging (5 km)	Level recovery training
Sunday	Training test: 25 km	

TOTAL	380 minutes (approximately 65 kilometers)

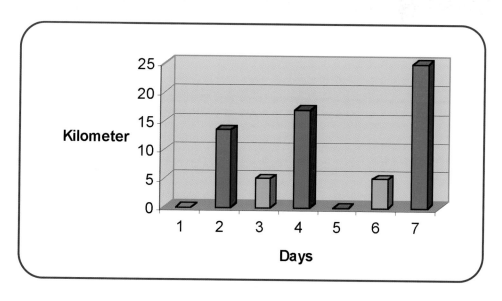

Week 11

This is the last week of thorough training. It is, however, of the greatest importance that before you start training this week, you are entirely recovered from Sunday's training test. The first days of this week entirely serve to recover from this 25 km run. For this reason, the total training volume this week will be rather limited.

Day	Training	Intensity description
Monday	Recovery day	
Tuesday	30 min jogging (5 km)	Level recovery training
Wednesday	Recovery day	
Thursday	15 min warming up 2 x 20 faster than running pace marathon, rec. 5 min running easily	Level AET3
	20 min easy running (14 km)	Level AET2
Friday	Recovery day	
Saturday	140 min easy running (23-24 km)	Level AET1
Sunday	30 min jogging (5 km)	Level recovery training
TOTAL	**280 minutes (approximately 47 kilometers)**	

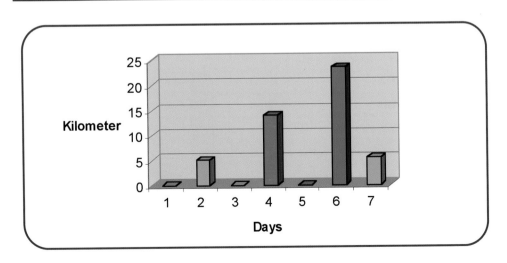

Week 12

During these last days before your marathon it really does not make any sense to train hard. You now have trained enough to successfully complete your marathon within the determined time of 4 hours. This last week is required to achieve maximum supercompensatio. This means that you scale back the training quantity drastically (tapering) to obtain maximum valuefrom all your past training sessions and to start the marathon entirely rested.

Day	Training	Intensity description
Monday	Recovery day	
Tuesday	40 min very easy running (6-7 km)	Level AET1
Wednesday	Recovery day	Level recovery training
Thursday	15 min warming up 3 x 5 min faster than running pace marathon, rec. 3 min running easily 15 min cooling down (8-9 km)	Level AET3
Friday	Recovery day	
Saturday	30 min jogging (5 km)	Level recovery training
Sunday	**Marathon**	

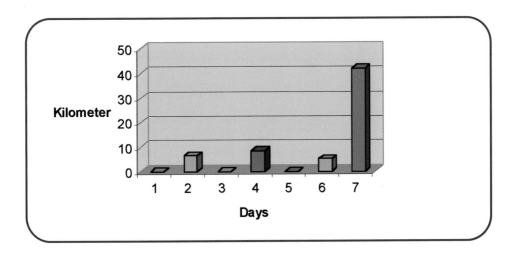

Important tips to reach your goal:

1. Do not start too fast. Do not get carried away by the tempo of other runners, but start slightly faster than the in-between time per kilometer needed to finish the marathon in 4 hours. A tempo of 5:30 is advisable to offset the typical slowdown during the second part of the race.

2. From the start, pay a lot of attention to fluid intake. Try to drink at every drink station. Be sure you replace not only fluid, but also energy by means of energy drinks.

A marathon in less than 3 hours

Breaking through the limit of three hours to complete a marathon is the dream of a lot of runners. Succeeding in this means a huge upgrade in your running status, the promotion of jogger to marathon runner.

It is not easy, however. You need, on average, three years of running experience to process the training required for this performance, without too great a risk of overload injuries.

There are two essential conditions to succeed in this performance:

1. You must be capable of processing a training volume of 80 to 100 kilometers per week.
2. Your best time over 10,000 meters must be lower than 38 minutes, preferably in the area of 36 minutes (3:36/kilometer). This requirement is no piece of cake at all! That is why the intensive training sessions must be aimed at gaining this time over 10 kilometers. It is advisable to regularly run a race over this distance during the preparation as well.

In spite of the fact that you must be able to run rather fast over 10 kilometers, the main component of training nevertheless remains Long Slow Distance training sessions.

Training during the preparation period

Just like in the preparation for a marathon in less than 4 hours, we now also assume that you will run the marathon in September or October. You can then fully enjoy the pleasant spring and summer months to complete your preparation.

But you will need to start preparing during the winter. Your training during the preparation period can look as follows:

January – February:

Weekly, four to five Long Slow Distance runs from 60-75 minutes. The tempo is kept relatively low; you always stay in the AET1-AET2 area. You accomplish a weekly total of approximately 60 to 65 kilometers.

If you feel like it you can participate in one or two cross-country races in February without specifically training for them.

If you do not run these races you can do a fartlek every two weeks, in which the tempo is forced up and scaled back instinctively. Do make sure that you absolutely do not go into the red during these training sessions. You go until the level "tempo-interval".

March – April:

The training volume is slightly forced up, especially by the fact that you run a LSD of 90-120 minutes each week. The tempo remains low, however, level AET1.

During another aerobic run of 1h 15 min, some faster parts are carried out, for example 2 x 3000 meters at a tempo of 3:45/kilometer. The recovery time between the faster parts amounts to 5 min easy jogging.

It is also a good idea to run one race of approximately 15 kilometers to a tempo of about 3:50/kilometer during these months.

May:

You are now running 6 times per week, and during the last week of the month you must be able to run 100 kilometers. During the three first weeks bring some tempo to the training sessions. For example, run once per week 3 x 3000 meters at a tempo of 3:40/kilometer.

TIP:
Make sure you insert a recovery week after every three weeks of training set-up!

The last 12 weeks before the marathon

The important **key-points** for this period are:
- A weekly training volume of 80 to 100 kilometers per week
- One to two road races of 21 to 30 kilometers at a tempo which is faster than the race tempo, meaning faster than 4:17/kilometer
- One intensive running training session per week with total distances of 10,000 meters, to a tempo of approximately 3:40 per repetition of 1000 meters, e.g., 8 x 1000 meters
- Weekly, one Long Slow Distance of two hours or longer, level AET1.
- One endurance run in which poprtions are run at a tempo faster than the marathon tempo
- The majority of the training is completed on a soft surface. It is, however, advisable from the 5th week onwards to run the longest training session of the week each time on a hard surface.

Week 1

To build up the total training volume to approximately 100 kilometers in a period of 12 weeks without too great a risk of overload injuries, you must be able to process approximately 75 kilometers of training during the first week. Although the emphasis is on the relatively slow aerobic runs, you should still carry out two more intensive training sessions. The training quantity which exceeds the threshold remains very restricted, however.

Day	Training	Intensity description
Monday	Recovery day	
Tuesday	3 km warm up 2 x 4000 meters, tempo 4:10/km, recovery 2 km jogging 3 km cool down Total: 16 km	Level AET3
Wednesday	5 km jogging	Level recovery training
Thursday	15 km easy running	Level AET2
Friday	3 km warm up, towards the end some short rhythm alternations 6 x 1000 meters, tempo 3:40/km, recovery each time 400 m jogging 3 km cool down Total: 14 km	Level tempo – interval
Saturday	5 km jogging	Level recovery training
Sunday	20 km, easy running	Level AET1
TOTAL	**75 km**	

Week 2

During this second week you build further on the same pattern as in the past week. You must keep in mind that both the training volume and the training intensity do yet not increase too drastically. Your total training volume increases by approximately 10 per cent. A larger increase strongly raises the risk of overload and fatigue.

Day	Training	Intensity description
Monday	Recovery day	
Tuesday	4 km warm up 3 x 3000 meters, tempo 4:10/km, recovery 1 km jogging 4 km cool down Total: 20 km	Level AET3
Wednesday	5 km jogging	Level recovery training
Thursday	15 km easy running	Level AET2
Friday	3 km warm up, towards end some short rhythm alternations 8 x 1000 meters, tempo 3:40/km, recovery each time 400 m jogging 3 km cool down Total: 16.8 km	Level tempo-interval
Saturday	5 km jogging	Level recovery training
Sunday	22 km, easy running	Level AET1
TOTAL	**83.8 km**	

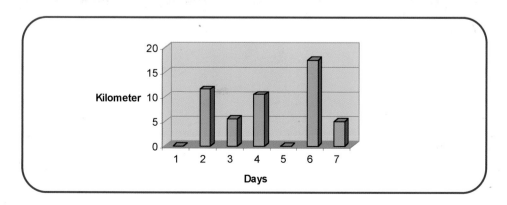

Week 3

At the end of this week you will have accomplished a total training volume of 90 kilometers. This is already a lot, also taking into account that on two of the six running days the tempo is higher than in the usual endurance runs. Therefore, pay attention to keeping a very low tempo during recovery running and during LSD training sessions!

Day	Training	Intensity description
Monday	Recovery day	
Tuesday	3 km warm up 5 x 2000 meters, tempo 4:00/km, recovery 1 km jogging 3 km cool down total: 20 km	Level AET3
Wednesday	8 km jogging	Level recovery training
Thursday	17 km easy running	Level AET2
Friday	3 km warm up, towards the end some short rhythm alternations 6 x 1500 meters, tempo 3:45/km, recovery each time 400 m jogging 3 km cool down Total: 17 km	Level tempo-interval
Saturday	5 km jogging	Level recovery training
Sunday	23 km easy running	Level AET1
TOTAL	**90 km**	

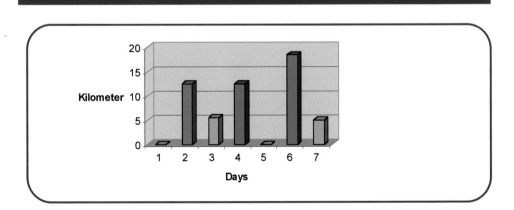

Week 4

This recovery week is quintessential. An extra recovery day is inserted, and both the training volume and the running intensity are scaled back drastically. Only once during this week should you bring higher intensity in your training, but purely instinctively (fartlek). If you should feel tired, then it is best to replace this training session by a short recovery training session.

Day	Training	Intensity description
Monday	Recovery day	
Tuesday	5 km jogging	Level recovery training
Wednesday	Recovery day	
Thursday	10 km easy running	Level AET2
Friday	5 km jogging	Level recovery training
Saturday	15 km light fartlek	Until level AET3
Sunday	20 km easy running	Level AET1
TOTAL	**55 km**	

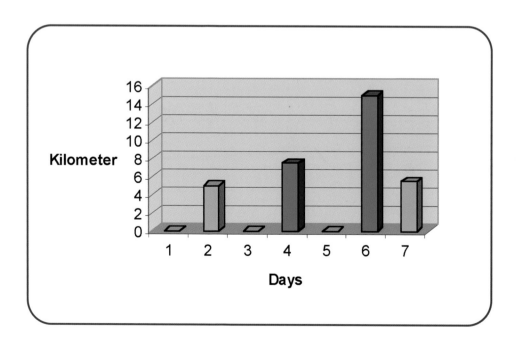

Week 5

It would very opportune to run a half-marathon at the end of this week at a tempo higher than the target marathon tempo. This will help you get in touch with the race rhythm, and this time in specific race circumstances. You can also test your fluid intake. Nevertheless it should certainly not be your intention to really go for it completely during this race. That is why the training volume does not really have to be scaled back before this race, which you should consider as a means to reach your eventual goal, and not as a goal in itself.

Day	Training	Intensity description
Monday	Recovery day	
Tuesday	3 km warm up 8 x 1000 meters, tempo alternating 3:40 – 3:45/km, recovery 200 meters jogging 3 km cool down Total 15.4 km	Level tempo-interval
Wednesday	20 km easy running	Level AET1
Thursday	5 km jogging	Level recovery training
Friday	12 km easy running	Level AET2
Saturday	5 km jogging	Level recovery training
Sunday	21 km race, tempo between 4:05 and 4:10/kilometer	

TOTAL	78.4 km

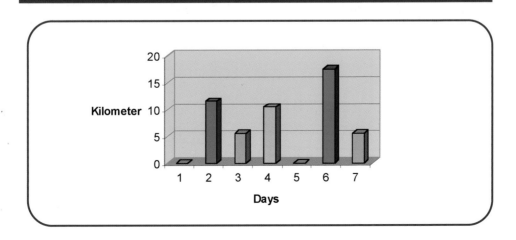

Week 6

Although you did not run at full speed during the half-marathon, you will nevertheless need three days to recover from the race. Because of this, the total training volume this week will be somewhat lower, and only one training session will be done at a higher intensity. On Thursday you should be ready again to do a more intensive training session. During all the other training sessions, the running pace must be low.

Day	Training	Intensity description
Monday	Recovery day	
Tuesday	10 km easy running	Level recovery training
Wednesday	Recovery day	
Thursday	3 km warm up 3000 meters, tempo 3:55/kilometer, 400 m jogging 2000 meters, tempo 3:45/kilometer, 400 m jogging 3 x 1000 meters, 3:40/kilometer, recovery each time 200 m jogging 3 km cool down Totally: 15.2 km	Level tempo-interval
Friday	15 km easy running	Level AET2
Saturday	5 km jogging	Level recovery training
Sunday	22 km easy running	Level AET1

TOTAL	67.2 km

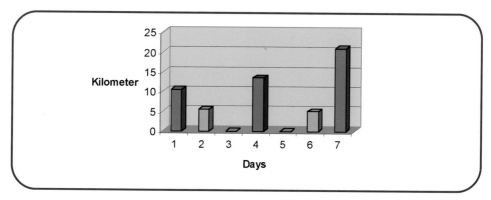

Week 7

During this week you return to the normal running pattern. On the one hand, the training volume is forced up to the maximum level, which you had already reached during the first three weeks of the training set-up. On the other hand, two more intensive training sessions are planned, of which one is carried out at an intensity above the threshold (tempo interval training).

Day	Training	Intensity description
Monday	Recovery day	
Tuesday	3 km warm up with 10 x 100 m. acceleration 3 x 3000 meters, progressively accelerate: 3:50 – 3:45 – 3:40/kilometer, recovery each time 400 m jogging 3 km cool down Total: 15.8 km	Level tempo-interval
Wednesday	20 km very easy running	Level AET1
Thursday	5 km jogging	Level recovery training
Friday	3 km warming up 10 x 1000 meters, tempo 4:05/kilometer, recovery each time 400 m jogging 3 km cooling down Total: 19.6 km	Level AET3
Saturday	5 km jogging	Level recovery training
Sunday	25 km easy running	Level AET1

TOTAL	**90.4 km**

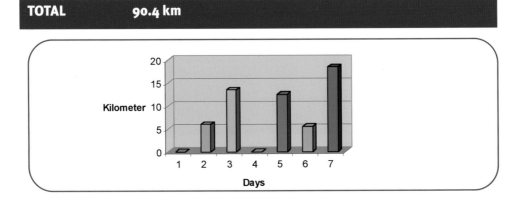

Week 8

At the end of this week you reach the turning point of 100 kilometers. Such a training volume on a weekly basis is a high load for the body. For this reason the second intensive run is replaced by a training session in which you introduce variation in your running pace purely instinctively. If you should feel tired, you can always replace this training session by a LSD run over the same distance.

Day	Training	Intensity description
Monday	Recovery day	
Tuesday	3 km warm up 10 x 200 meters, alternatively "rolling" (36 – 38) and jogging 400 meters jogging 8 x 1000 meters, alternating 3:55 – 3:35/km recovery each time 400 meters jogging 3 km cool down, very relaxed Total: 19.2 kilometers	Level tempo-interval
Wednesday	10 km easy running	Level AET2
Thursday	25 km easy running	Level AET1
Friday	6 km jogging	Level recovery training
Saturday	15 km fartlek	Until level AET3
Sunday	25 km easy running	Level AET1

TOTAL	100.2 km

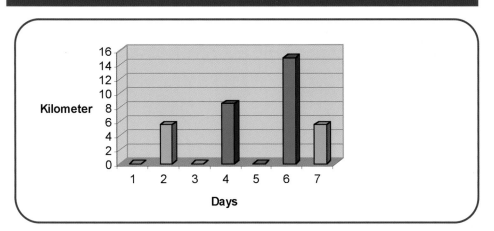

Week 9

The past weeks have undoubtedly left their marks. Your muscles probably do not feel supple anymore, and perhaps you will notice that your heart rate does not always react as well to the implementation of tempo alternation. It is absolutely necessary to scale back the overall training drastically during this week to let your muscles recover and let past training labor produce its maximum value.

Day	Training	Intensity description
Monday	Recovery day	
Tuesday	6 km jogging	Level recovery training
Wednesday	Recovery day	
Thursday	12 km easy running	Level AET2
Friday	5 km jogging	Level recovery training
Saturday	15 km light fartlek	Until level AET3
Sunday	22 km easy running	Level AET1
TOTAL	**60 km**	

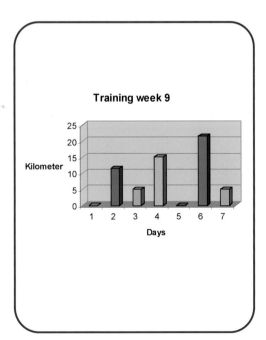

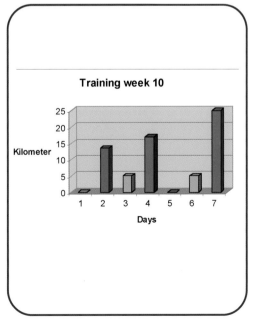

Week 10

This is the last tough training week in your training set-up for completing a marathon in less than three hours. Beside the two normal training sessions in which you train to a higher running speed, you now do for the first (and only) time a training session longer than 25 kilometers. It is best to restrict yourself to not more than 30 kilometers. If you force up the running distance still further, there is a risk that you destruct more than you construct! You must be able to complete this very LSD run without too many problems. Test your fluid intake during this training session once more.

Day	Training	Intensity description
Monday	Recovery day	
Tuesday	3 km warm up with 10 x 100 m acceleration 2 x 5000 meters, progressively accelerate: 4:00 – 3:50/kilometer, recovery 800 m jogging 3 km cool down Total: 16.8 km	Level tempo-interval
Wednesday	22 km easy running	Level AET1
Thursday	6 km jogging	Level recovery training
Friday	3 km warm up 4000 meters, 4 min a kilometer, 400 meters jogging 2 x 2000 meters, 3:50/kilometer, recovery 400 meters jogging 2 x 1000 meters, 3:35/km, recovery 400 meters jogging 3 km cool down total: 17.6 km	Level AET3 Level tempo-interval
Saturday	6 km jogging	Level recovery training
Sunday	30 km easy running	Level AET1
TOTAL	**98.4 km**	

Week 11

Now the "tapering off" starts. The global weekly training volume is scaled back, although there must nevertheless still be a number of LSD training sessions programmed. One training session in which you train instinctively to a higher intensity is also still planned.

Keep in mind that in case of fatigue, rest has a better impact than an extra training session. You should not be afraid to replace a training session by a complete recovery day if you feel tired!

Day	Training	Intensity description
Monday	Recovery day	
Tuesday	20 km easy running	Level AET1
Wednesday	6 km jogging	Level recovery training
Thursday	18 km with instinctively tempo alternations (fartlek)	Until level AET3
Friday	Recovery day	
Saturday	25 km easy running	Level AET1
Sunday	5 km jogging	Level recovery training
TOTAL	**74 km**	

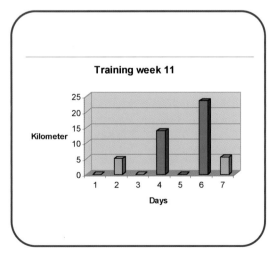

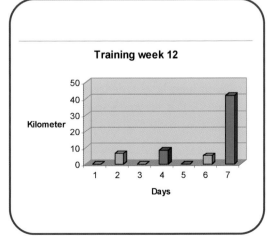

Week 12

During this last week you should train very little. Although some running training is still required to keep your condition on a good level, you can now also replace a day programmed for easy running with a complete recovery day. It now boils down to replenishing your energy supplies fully and arriving completely rested to the start of the race.

Day	Training	Intensity description
Monday	Recovery day	
Tuesday	12 km with light rhythm changes	Fartlek to level AET3
Wednesday	5 km jogging	Level recovery training
Thursday	12 km easy running	Level AET2
Friday	Recovery day	
Saturday	6 km very relaxed running	Level recovery training
Sunday	**Marathon**	

Calculating your possible end time in the marathon

Wouldn't it be nice if you could determine your marathon finish time in advance?
A commonly used method for this is that you multiply end time of the half-marathon (in minutes) by a certain coefficient. This coefficient can be between 2.1 and 2.5, depending on your level of conditioning.

If you are better trained your coefficient will be lower. Top runners can use a coefficient of 2.1. A time in a half-marathon of 63 minutes could then result in a marathon time of approximately 2 hours and 12 minutes.

If you have little experience with the marathon and your training has been relatively limited, it is advisable to presume that your time will be your end time on the half-marathon multiplied by 2.5.

A time of 1:45 for the half-marathon means you can expect a marathon time of 4:22.

CHAPTER 10

Running faster with correct nutrition

As mentioned before, your performance level is determined by numerous factors. All these factors are essential to reaching your individual maximum performance level. One of the most important performance-determining factors is your nutrition pattern.

The importance of a good nutrition pattern

To get better insight in the importance of a good nutrition pattern, we need to again take a look at the energy supplies of the body.

The two main energy sources of the body are carbohydrates and fatty acids. In extreme circumstances proteins can also be called upon as an energy source. In this last case, however, the muscles are literally being demolished. It should be clear that this last case would lead to a loss of conditioning within a very short period.

When are fats applied as an energy source and when carbohydrates?
During efforts of very low intensity, fatty acids are almost exclusively used as an energy source. As the effort intensity increases, the share of carbohydrates will increase as an energy supplier, and eventually, during very intensive effort, energy is still exclusively provided by oxidation of carbohydrates.

These carbohydrates have been piled up in the body in the form of glycogen in the muscles and in the liver, but the stock is limited. It is commonly believed that during very intensive efforts the carbohydrate supply will be used up after approximately 90 minutes.

Research has shown that after intensive training sessions, an average of only 5% of muscle glycogen used during training are replaced each hour. Complete exhaustion of muscle glycogen therefore requires 20 hours before the muscle glycogen stocks are completely replenished.

The stock of fatty acids in the body, on the other hand, is seemingly inexhaustible. The disadvantage of "fatty acids energy" versus "carbohydrates energy" is that the energy supply from fatty acids gets started more slowly, and that for the same quantity of oxygen taken in, less energy is produced when compared to carbohydrates.

Guidelines for efforts at low intensity

When you train to low intensity, for example the Long Slow Distance, fatty acids are mostly applied to an energy source. Since there is a sufficiently large stock of this energy source in the body, you can keep up a normal nutrition pattern, which consists on average of 60% carbohydrates, 25% fats and 15% proteins.

Replenishing fluid loss

For such training sessions it is, however, of great importance that fluid loss is always sufficiently compensated, during and especially after training. Drinking during training sessions is not easy. Belts with bottle holders exist to help you carry fluids during the run training. This is not really comfortable however. Another possibility is to plan the training session so a half-way training stop can be inserted to drink.

The body has a built in temperature regulator at its disposal, and it strives to keep your body temperature constantly on 36 to 37° Celsius. When running your body temperature will increase, so by means of perspiration the body will try to keep the internal body temperature on level.

It is not the sweat secretion in itself that ensures the cooling of the body, but the vaporization of this sweat. It is obvious that sweat vaporization is not only strongly influenced by the external temperature, but also by the humidity level of the air. Sweat vaporization in warm and dry weather will cause cooling of the body sooner than in warm and wet weather. The body temperature will also increase much more rapidly in warm than in cool weather. This is especially important for efforts of long duration. For short-term efforts a temperature of 23° to 30° Celsius seems to be most suitable. For long-term efforts the ideal temperature is about 18° Celsius.

Abundant perspiration may have an important damaging impact on the body. Research has shown that just a 1% hydration loss leads to performance loss. A 3% to 5% loss can equal a fall of 10 to 30% of the performance capacity. Why is this the case?

By reduction of the fluid volume, blood becomes less liquid. Because of this, the heart will pump less effectively. Less oxygen can be transported to the working muscles and less sweat will be produced.

There will be less sweat vaporization, which will lead to the body temperature still increasing. Thus for endurance sportsmen the rectal temperature can rise in extreme cases to 40° C/104°F and even still higher. A temperature of 41°C/106°F is very dangerous and can cause irreparable damage to the liver, kidneys and brain.

Overheating can lead to heat cramps, heat exhaustion and eventually heat collapse.
Heat cramps generally occur in the calves when a person sweats exuberantly without compensating for the fluid loss.
Heat exhaustion is a further stage and has the same cause. In this case, activities must be immediately stopped.
    Heat collapse is the most critical form of overheating and is not always preceded by cramps or exhaustion. Heat collapse blocks the thermoregulating mechanisms of the body, and as a result, body temperature will strongly increase. A fast admission to a hospital is vital. Vital aid must include a fast cooling by water, ice or air.
    It is wrong to think that overheating can only occur in endurance races in warm and wet weather. Long-term, tough efforts in moderate climate conditions can increase the body temperature drastically.

Guidelines for training sessions at average intensity

During training sessions when the intensity is a little higher, fatty acids are still used as the primary energy source. Depending on the training intensity, however, the share of carbohydrates used gradually and consistently increases. Replenishing the fluid lost by means of thirst quenchers is advisable here, to compensate for the lost minerals and to supplement the glycogen reserves. Otherwise, normal healthy nutrition should be sufficient.

Guidelines for training sessions at high intensity

For this type of training sessions, your body mainly appeals to carbohydrates as an energy supplier. It is best to have already replenished carbohydrates burned during training sessions or races lasting longer than one hour, in order to avoid an encounter with "the wall" or "the man with the hammer". The so-called **energy drinks** are very important here, because they allow you to replenishing carbohydrates burned in an easy manner during training or races. Of course, you still need to use thirst quenchers as well to compensate the fluid loss.

Guidelines after intensive training or races

After an intensive training session or after a race, supplementing the carbohydrate stock is very important. You should start with this supplement within 30 minutes after training. Research has shown that maximum recovery can be reached by a combination of carbohydrates and protein, in a proportion of 50%-50%. Most **recovery drinks** meet these conditions.

Protein ensures that the negative nitrogen balance arisen from the intensive effort is neutralized. Preferably the first intake is liquid (recovery drink). Later you can switch to solid food, such as rice, pasta, bread etc. The share of the carbohydrates in solid nutrition can be now forced up to 70%.

Food having a high share of carbohydrates has a double function.
First, it leads to an increase of blood sugar, which helps to replenish exhausted muscles.

Secondly the body reacts to this increase of blood glucose with an insulin response to again decrease blood glucose. This insulin response is anabolic (muscle developing) because insulin stimulates the shaping of muscle protein.

Practically, this means you must start within 15 to 30 minutes after intensive training with the intake of 100g carbohydrates in combination with protein, followed by 100g carbohydrates every 2 hours following. It is advisable at the first and the second intake to use liquid carbohydrates (recovery drinks) because these are processed more rapidly than carbohydrates in solid form. Afterwards you can switch to food.

You can obtain100 g of carbohydrates from, for instance: 150 g muesli, 150 g raisins, 140 g spaghetti (raw), 350 g cooked rice, 500 g potatoes (cooked), 5 bananas, 200 g dried figs, 250 g whole-wheat bread.

Note:

If carbohydrates must be taken in fast you should choose products with a high glycemic index (GI). The GI is a measurement for the speed with which carbohydrates are incorporated in the body and the increase of blood sugar quality that results. Products having a high GI include white bread, whole-wheat bread, cornflakes, muesli, bananas and raisins. Pastas only have an average GI.

When you do not replenish your carbohydrate stock after intensive training sessions and races, your recovery goes slower. After some days of intensive training you feel spiritless and your training output decreases. It is clear that all this has a very negative impact on your final performance capacity.

Nutrition before the race

Days before the race

During the days preceding a tough race, for example a marathon, the energy supply (carbohydrate stock) in the body can be intensified by means of adapting nutrition and training. Because of this, fatigue can be postponed during the race.

Practically speaking, you operate as follows:
- train intensively up to 5 to 6 days before the race
- then gradually reduce the training quantity and quality (tapering)
- eat meals with a high share of carbohydrates during the last 3 days before the race

By following these directives muscle glycogen can exceed 20 to 40% above the normal level.
The day before the race a total of 600-800 g carbohydrates must be taken.

Just before the race

It is advisable having a meal with a high share of carbohydrates (150-200 g carbohydrates) between 3 and 6 hours prior to the race. This way the food has been digested by the time you start. Afterwards it is better not to eat carbohydrates anymore, because too many carbohydrates in the blood could bring about an insulin reaction. Insulin is the hormone that keeps your carbohydrate stock in your blood on the right level. Due to this insulin reaction your sugar level may drop so much that you could feel tired and washed-out.

Carbohydrate intake just before the start of the race (5 to 10 minutes) causes no problem because these carbohydrates are only incorporated after the race is underway. During intense efforts there is no insulin reaction.

In warm and humid circumstances it can also be useful to build a fluid reserve. You can do this by drinking approximately 500ml water or thirst quencher during the last half-hour before the race.

Guidelines for healthy nutrition

As mentioned before, the nutrition of an endurance athlete must comprise 60% carbohydrates (during intensive training days even up to 70%), 20-25% fats and 15% protein.

Generally speaking, the following products are advisable: lots of vegetables, preferably uncooked; a lot of fruit; pasta, rice, potatoes, brown bread; chicken and fish; skimmed and semi-skimmed dairy products; muesli and other cereals.

The following products are not recommended: fat meat products; fried food; whole dairy products; salt; excessive sweets (cakes, cookies, chocolate...) ; alcohol ; crisps; ....

Furthermore you must pay much attention to the fluid intake during the day. This means that during the day you must regularly drink water apart from training. Water is preferred to coffee, because coffee has a water secreting impact. The use of coffee must be therefore limited. Moreover coffee blocks the intake of Vitamin C.

TIP:

Particularly at breakfast, take sufficient Kcal to provide the energy for the training labor coming. It is also best to eat some snacks now and then in order to prevent feeling hungry. At night it is best to eat less.

What about fats?

Your nutrition is built around the intake of carbohydrates. This does not mean, however, that fats must be avoided systematically. On the contrary, if you train intensely and regularly you should not be afraid to consciously eat fats at regular times.

Fats ensure, by means of LDL-cholesterol, the production of the steroids, includingthe anabolic hormone testosterone. A light body weight and little body fat are connected in several studies with men having a very low testosterone level. This results in a slowed down recovery from training labor.

Although saturated fats cannot be avoided completely, unsaturated fats are preferred. These are found in, among other things, vegetable oil, nuts, seeds and fat fish.

How much do you really have to eat?

The answer to this question is primarily determined by the training labor performed. One hour of easy endurance training corresponds with approximately 600 Kcal energy usage, one hour of very intensive run training with 800 Kcal.

An athlete of 70 kilograms consumes, without training, approximately 2700 Kcal daily. If this runner trains 2 hours quietly, his usage amounts to approximately 3800 to 4000 Kcal.

As mentioned before, the quantity of carbohydrates you must take in daily depends on your training labor performed. On average this need can be calculated as follows:
- during recovery days: 4 to 5 g CH/kilogram body weight
- during training days (1 to 2 hours duration training, or 1 hour very intensive training): 7 to 8 g CH/kilogram body weight

An athlete weighing 70 kilograms must thus take approximately 500 g carbohydrates during tough training days.

	Kcal	Protein	Fat	Carbohydrates
Banana	88	1	0	20
Apple	50	0	0	12
Orange	47	1	0	11
Kiwi	40	1	0	9
Muesli without sugar	390	11	8	68
Muesli with sugar	396	11	11	64
Oat meal	363	13	7	62
Cornflakes	370	7	1	84
Muesli bar	440	5	17	67
Milk skimmed	37	4	0.1	5
Milk semi-skimmed	46	4	1.5	5
Milk whole	63	4	3.4	5
Yogurt skimmed	35	4	0.1	4
Yogurt semi-skimmed	49	4	1.5	5
Yogurt whole	85	5	4.5	6
Brown bread	248	10	3	45
Whole-wheat bread	222	9	3	41
Margarine	730	0	80	1
Cheese 20 % fat	245	34	12	0
Cheese 50% fat	370	23	31	0
Ham, raw	199	23	12	0
Chicken roll	166	24	7	2
Chocolate sprinklings	431	6	17	64
Marmalade	112	0	0	28

Caption above table: **Share of Kcal, protein, fats and carbohydrates of some common nutrients by 100 g**

	Kcal	Protein	Fat	Carbohydrates
Share of Kcal, protein, fats and carbohydrates of some common nutrients by 100 g				
Spaghetti raw	350	12	2	71
Spaghetti cooked	94	3	1	19
Pizza, cheese and tomato	211	10	1	26
Rice unboiled	346	7	1	78
Rice cooked	147	3	0	33
Potato, cooked	76	2	0	17
Fries	310	5	15	38
Cauliflower, raw	14	2	0	2
Carrots, raw	11	1	0	2
Endive, raw	5	1	0	0
Peas, cooked	60	4	0	11
Raw vegetables	14	1	0	2
Tomatoes	11	1	0	2
Leek, raw	24	1	0	0
Vegetable soup	34	1	2	3
Cod fish, cooked	105	23	1	0
Salmon	271	28	18	0
Chicken filet	158	31	4	0
Turkey filet	158	31	4	0
Breakfast bacon	404	15	38	0
Pork tenderloin	147	28	4	0
Beefsteak	139	27	3	1
Roast beef	167	28	6	1
Pudding, vanilla	114	4	3	19
Ice	182	3	9	22

Do protein supplements have to be taken?

In contrast to the intake of carbohydrates, you can assume that a normal nutrition pattern always contains sufficient protein.

An endurance sportsman has a daily protein need of approximately 1.3 g/kilogram. An athlete weighing 70 kilograms needs approximately 91 g protein per day. If you know that a piece of chicken weighing approximately 200 g already provides almost half of the daily amount, it should be clear that you do not have to strive for extra protein supplementing. Besides the necessary protein intake (combined with carbohydrates) right after an intense training session or after a race, slight supplementing can be considered only at the beginning of a new training set-up.

Protein is the building material of the body. Protein is called up as an energy source of the body in extreme cases, viz. at complete and continuing exhaustion of the glycogen stocks.

What to do when being overweight?

A lot of athletes struggle with being overweight during the relative recovery period. They had to restrain from too many things during the race period, and therefore they slacken the reins too much at a certain point. Sometimes it is very difficult to lose the weight again.

Following a strict diet to get to your ideal weight is being strictly discouraged. A too-high negative energy balance (more energy is consumed than is taken in) leads after some time to reduction of the muscles (protein is used as energy supplier), prevents the recovery of the body and therefore leads to overtraining, bringing along a significant drop in performance potential.

TIPS against being overweight

- Limit weight increase during the relative recovery period. It makes no sense to eat without brakes during this period. Stop at 2 to 3 kilograms above the ideal weight.
- If overweight, start early with an adapted nutrition pattern avoiding useless nutrition such as sweets and soda. If necessary you should strive for a slightly negative energy balance, so that the ideal weight can be reached very gradually. This slightly negative energy balance is only necessary when, in spite of the adapted nutrition pattern and increasing training labor, the body weight does not decrease. Maximum 2 kilograms per month seems a safe amount of weight to lose.
- You best lose weight by means of long easy endurance training sessions. During these run training sessions, fatty acids are oxidized. Intensive training sessions mainly oxidize carbohydrates.

- When following a diet you must always pay enough attention to the fact that the diet is not done at the expense of carbohydrates. Especially intensive training labor requires permanent replenishing of the carbohydrates under all circumstances. For reasons mentioned above, fat must keep its place in your nutrition as well.

6% body fat

In recent years, the fixed idea has arisen that a runner only stands sharp if his body fat is reduced to 6% or less. This is absolutely untrue, because body fat percentage is very personal. Some athletes have, by nature, a very low body fat percentage. For them it is not difficult to reach 6%. Other athletes have, by nature, a much higher body fat percentage. They can reach 6% only after following a very strict diet, in which they always show a negative energy balance. They take in too few carbohydrates, and as a result the energy stocks in their muscles are no longer replenished after intense training. Moreover, in the nutrition pattern of these athletes there is generally no room for fatty acids. The consequence often is a spectacular drop of their performance potential. Research has shown that too abrupt weight loss leads to reduction of the aerobic and anaerobic capacity, of absolute strength and of strength endurance. Following a very strict diet is, therefore, catastrophic for most athletes.

The ideal weight of an athlete cannot be captured in a postulated weight or fat percentage. An athlete knows from experience when he is "sharp", and which weight he must reach to achieve his best performance. If an athlete trains well, and takes into account the elementary nutrition directives mentioned above, strict diets are not necessary.

How about nutrition supplements and other preparations?

Concerning nutrition supplements and preparations, it is difficult to still see the forest for the trees.

Some supplements, however, do seem to help your training:

- Arginine and ornitine:
  Amino acids which, when administered in sufficiently large quantities, stimulate the pituitary gland. Because of this, the production of the body growth hormone is stimulated. The growth hormone improves recovery after effort.

- Glutamine:
  An amino acid which reduces muscle demolition and reinforces the immune system.

- Antioxidants:
  In the body, as a result of the metabolism and energy production, free radicals are being produced. These free radicals are, among other things, responsible for cardiac diseases, some forms of cancers, ageing and muscular ache after effort. Research has also shown that training increases the amount of free radicals. Antioxidants are substances which neutralize the damaging functioning of free radicals. Thus the damage to muscle cells would be less for sportsmen who take supplementing antioxidants than for those who do not take these supplements.

- Vitamins and mineral supplements:
  Quite a lot of athletes take such supplements, and generally in very large quantities. These supplements are necessary because most people eat too little fruit and vegetables. An athlete who eats 4 to 6 pieces of fruit and fresh vegetables every day, does not need these expensive preparations.

- Vitamin C:
  This vitamin nevertheless demands particular attention for two reasons. On the one hand it belongs to the antioxidants, and on the other hand, it has been proven that vitamin C raises the resistance of the body against infections. A runner who trains intensely has an inferior resistance against infections, because the effort has decreased the resistance against these infections. Vitamin C raises this resistance to a sufficiently high level. One to two grams/day during periods of intense training and races seems suitable. When infections arise some doctors even prescribe five grams/day.

- Iron:
  Iron supplement is only significant if there is an iron shortage, i.e. too low ferritine levels. Many athletes systematically take iron preparations, even without a shortage being established. This makes no sense, since it can be dangerous for your health, as surplus iron piles up in the spinal cord and in organs such as the liver.

CHAPTER 11

Losing weight through running

On important reason to start jogging is that you are not at all, or not entirely, satisfied with your body weight. Even being just a little overweight can be enough to make you feel uncomfortable in your own body. One way to get rid of this problem can be taking up a jogging program. Jogging thus becomes no more or no less a means to reach a more ideal body weight.

But what is your ideal weight, and how efficient can jogging be to reach this weight?

Methods to determine the ideal weight

Although most top long distance runners are slim and tall, we see among the mass of joggers runners in all measurements and weights. Many people with a rather robust appearance can nevertheless run surprisingly fast.

This is due to various muscle types. So is there really an ideal body weight, and an ideal running weight, for everyone? There are some methods with which you can try to quantify the ideal body weight.

Body fat percentage

The measuring of the body fat percentage is the traditional means to determine whether the runner stands sufficiently "sharp," i.e., if he has reached his ideal competition weight.

The body fat percentage is generally determined by means of measuring skin creases in 4 different places: the biceps muscle, the triceps, under the scapula and above the hip.
The sum of all skin creases measured provides an estimate of the of body fat percentage .

These measurements and interpretations are not always that precise, because the test measuring demands much expertise, the quantity of subcutaneous fat varies according to age, sex and race, and the compression of the skin creases is age-based.

It is essential that these measurements are always carried out in the same manner and by the same person so that the evolution of body fat percentage can be determined over time.

For adult men a fat percentage between 12 and 18% is considered to be normal, for women it is higher, between 17 and 22%. Finding trained runners fat percentages between 6 and 10% is not unusual.

These standards allow (too) large variation. A person of 75kg with a body fat percentage of 18% has approximately 4.5kg more body fat than just as heavy person with 12% body fat. Despite this great difference, both will be classified as normal on the standard scale. The standard scale presented therefore does not allow determining the optimum body weight.

Body length in centimeters minus 110

According to this rule of thumb the ideal weight of a person of 1.80 m. should be 70 kilograms.
To find out whether this is correct or not, it is foremost important to be aware that everyone naturally tends to a certain body type, also called *somatotype*. Three body types are commonly to be distinguished:

- *the ectomorph type*
  The characteristics of this body type are a long, narrow figure, little developed muscles, a long chest, thin limbs and shoulders hanging down.

- *the endomorph type*
  characterized as a rather squat figure, red complexion, a big belly and tendency to obesity.

- *the mesomorph type*
  This is the muscular body type with a highly developed skeleton, broad shoulders, narrow pelvis.

In real life, the external appearance will be stipulated by a mixture of characteristics of two types, in which the characteristics of one certain type will be dominant.

It goes without saying that the ideal weight of someone who belongs to the mesomorph type will differ from the ideal weight of an endomorph type.

Generally speaking, we see that good long distance runners are tall and slim, and tend to the ectomorph type, often combined with a slightly mesomorph influence.

Body-Mass index (BMI)

Research has shown that there is a rather constant correlation between weight and the length squared. This correlation is expressed in Body-Mass index (BMI), body weight is divided by body length squared.

Example: a person of 1.80 m weighing 70 kg has a BMI of 70/(1.80*1.80) = 21.6.

By means of this index you can get insight in the degree of obesity of a certain person. Following standard scale is used:

BMI< 20:	Underweight
BMI = 20 tot 25:	Normal weight
BMI = 25 tot 30:	Overweight
BMI > 30:	Obesity

As the BMI increases, there is also an increase in health risk. From BMI 25 and onwards the risk of possible heart disease is said to increase significantly.
Questions about this classification following BMI nevertheless need to be raised.

First the somatotype is not taken into account. A very muscular type having a length of 1.80m and a weight of 85kg has a BMI of 26.3. An untrained person having the same length and a weight of 76 kg has a BMI of 23.4, whereas his mass of fat is probably absolutely and relatively much larger than the one of the muscular type.
Secondly the standard scale allows too large a margin in the same category. A trained person measuring 1.80m having a weight of 70kg has a BMI of 21.6. Suppose this person stops training, no longer pays attention to his nutrition and puts on 7kg (fat mass), his BMI of 23.7, which is still considered acceptable according the classification.
Because weight loss is often equated with performance profit, the longing for this weight loss can take obsessive forms among runners. When carried to a drastic extent, we call this anorexia. Such eating disorders are not only a threat to your health; they also strongly undermine the performance potential of the runner.

Conclusion
It does not seem to be possible to determine a generally applicable standard for the ideal body weight. Weight depends too much on factors such as a body composition and age. Reference values such as length minus 110, BMI and fat percentage are certainly indicative when striving towards the ideal weight. How you look and feel continue to play a large role in determining whether someone meets his ideal weight.

Weight loss through running

A lot of runners think that they will lose more weight if they run faster, and if they sweat more during running training. This is wrong.

First of all, as mentioned before, the fat metabolism is particularly stimulated during slow, long duration training sessions.

Fats	Fats	Fats	Fats	
Carbohydrates		Carbohydrates	Carbohydrates	Carbohydrates
	Carbohydrates	Carbohydrates		
AET1	AET2	AET3	Tempo interval training	Intensive interval training

Share of the oxidation of fat and of carbohydrates in the energy supply for the different types of training

If you want to lose weight, it is advisable to opt for LSD training sessions, rather than running training sessions at high intensity. As the intensity is higher, fatty acids will be spared and the oxidation of carbohydrates will be addressed much more.

Weight loss cannot be pursued by means of perspiration, either. Sweat is a thermoregulating mechanism. This means that you keep your body temperature on level by means of vaporization of sweat. Vaporization of sweat on the skin ensures cooling. This fluid loss must be replenished after training as soon as possible.

You should not exaggerate the weight loss you can expect by means of jogging.

One kilogram of fat corresponds to an energetic value of 7000 Kcal. If you know that a one hour easy run approximately amounts to 600 Kcal, you should jog, roughly speaking, 12 hours to lose 1 kilogram. Especially for joggers and recreational runners, these 12 hours mean a time span that could be spread out over three to five weeks!

It is very important therefore that you also spend much attention on a healthy and balanced nutrition pattern in addition to run training to obtain any weight loss. Generally there is no problem here, because people who run will automatically pay sufficient attention to a healthy nutrition pattern.

CHAPTER 12

Overtraining

What is overtraining?

Running is a passion, and is literally addictive. Quite soon you will compare distances and times, with yourself, and with others. How long? How far? Quicker and further. You always want more.

You may feel that you trained well and extensively, but suddenly your results stagnate and later slacken. Often this prompts you to train even harder, devouring still more kilometers without any improvement. On the contrary, performances will often decline even further. How is that possible?

To answer this question we need to analyze the term **training**.

Training is administering systematic physical stimulations to the body, taking into account the capacity of the body. These stimulations bring about changes in the body which lead, when considering the correct proportion of effort and recovery, to an increase of the performance capacity.

In this definition there are some important data:

- **Taking into account the capacity of the body:**
  every athlete has a certain training capacity. This capacity can vary from one day to the next. Insufficient sleep, bad nutrition, illness, or stress can all reduce the capacity of the body.

Not every runner has the same capacity. Some athletes can perform more training labor than others. Running is indeed a very straining sport. Therefore it makes no sense to just copy training set-ups of other successful athletes.

It is far more important to take into account the training principles applied by good athletes, and apply these principles while considering your own capacity. It is not so that the runner with the largest capacity by definition also obtains the best results. Some athletes can achieve better results with less training than athletes who train harder and more frequently.

Overtraining arises if the training stimuli are stronger than the individual's capacity. It is possible to distinguish *qualitative overtraining* and *quantitative overtraining*.

The cause for **qualitative overtraining** is typically found in the intensity of the training pivots, i.e. you train too intensively. In **quantitative overtraining**, on the other hand, the training volume is too large, the training duration is too long. Overtraining often appears as a combination of these two forms.

Therefore it is very important that training intensity and training volume are forced up gradually. In the beginning of a training set-up you should first pay attention to gradually forcing up training volume. In other words, you must always strive for extensive basic endurance (aerobic endurance) before starting to train more intensively. You constantly have to give your body the opportunity to adapt to a rising training workload. Intensifying the training workload too suddenly, qualitatively or quantitatively, leads to a drop in performance level after a while.

At that moment you are very susceptible to overload injuries. Especially when starting a new training program, after some time off or after a tough race period, you should handle your training with care. Even for the best-trained athletes, there is a shaky balance between performance improvement and overtraining.

- **Consider the correct proportion effort – recovery:**
  It may sound strange, but training itself decreases performance levels. By the end of the training session you are tired and not able to repeat the session. A positive training impact is possible only after a sufficiently long recovery period. This mechanism is called the **principle of supercompensation**.

The principle of supercompensation

The next diagram explains this principle and makes clear that without recovery no performance improvement can be obtained:

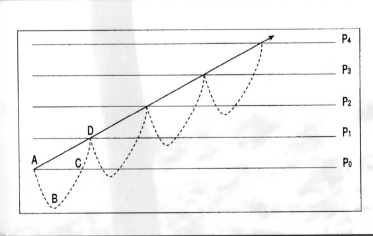

PO, P1, P2, P3, P4... *different performance levels*

AB: drop of the performance level as a result of training fatigue

BC: the rise of the performance level during recovery period is insufficient due to insufficient recovery time. A new training stimulus was inserted too early. As a result of this there is no supercompensation and we see a drop, instead of a rise, of the performance level.

From this diagram clearly shows that a next training stimulation must be given on the top of the supercompensation.

Here you meet however the great difficulty: when have you recovered sufficiently to train again, and how intensive can this training be? In other words: how much time do you need after a certain training session to reach supercompensation?

The time to reach supercompensation is determined by a number of elements

- *The nature of the training session:*
  As the training session is more intensive, the recovery phase lasts longer. A LSD run demands thus less recovery time than intensive interval training.

- *The degree of being trained of the athlete:*
  A well trained runner needs less recovery time after a LSD run of 2 hours than a less well trained runner after an easy run of 1 hour. Well trained runners can feel already fully recovered from a LSD run after they have taken a shower.

- *The mental state of the athlete:*
  There is a clear link between the mental and physical condition. You recover much slower of an effort when you are stressed than when you are relaxed.

- *Other factors such as nutrition and sleep:*
  The correct nutrition with attention to the intake of carbohydrates, possibly in combination with amino acids, both during training and after training (see further) is essential for an optimum recovery phase. A normal sleep pattern also has an important role. Because of a range of hormonal processes it is important to go to bed in time and to get up in time as well. The testosterone quality in blood (testosterone is a constructive hormone) experiences an increase during the night, reaching a peak in the morning. A normal night's rest optimizes the anabolic functioning of this hormone.

- *A correct medical support:*
  In which possible shortages are swiftly completed after blood analysis (e.g. iron, vit B12 etc.).

Indications in order to determine the top of supercompensation

- *Your subjective feeling:*
  If you feel tired, you will certainly not yet have reached the top of supercompensation. There is, of course, "normal" fatigue" after a rough training session. Sometimes fatigue lingers, even after a normal night's rest, and your legs feel sluggish and even painful while training. Continuing to complete your training does not make sense. You must always keep in mind that a tired body is not trainable; on the contrary you can only reverse the training effect by training more. Runners are very passionate, and therefore it is often hard to admit you feel tired.

- *Blood analyses:*
  By means of a series of parameters, such as the number of red blood cells, hemoglobin quality, the haematocrite value (the proportion of the number of red blood cells to the total plasma volume) etc., doctors can establish whether or not you are wearing yourself out by training. Such analyses are however rather expensive and can only be carried out a few times per year.

- *Submaximal or maximal tests:*
  The performance level during these tests, paired with other parameters such as the curve of the heart rate during the test, can offer an idea of the recovery process.

- *The heart rate during training:*
  If you are used to training and using a heart rate monitor you can observe quite quickly whether your training heart rate is "normal" based on the effort made. If you realize that your heart rate is higher than usual, this can be an indication that you have not yet recuperated sufficiently from the preceding training session. It is also possible that a low heart rate, or the feeling that you cannot increase the heart rate, indicates fatigue (see further).

- *A clear insight in the nature of the training sessions undertaken*
  It is advisable to keep a training diary. When you are well aware of the type of training you have done, you can adjust, in case of fatigue, your recovery phase.

The next table shows the recovery time needed in function of the nature of the training session.

From this table you can deduce, among other things, that you have to wait at least 3 days after an intensive training session before you may do the same session again.
All this does not mean that you cannot train during the recovery phase after intensive

Recovery time	Type of work load			
	Aerobic	85-95% Aerobic-Anaerobic	95-100% Anaerobic	Strength
During the effort	Intensity 60-70%			
Immediate but incomplete recovery		After 1.5 -2 h	After 2 h	After 2 h
90-95% recovery	At intensity 75-80% after 12 h	After 12 h	After 12-18 h	After 18 h
Complete recovery	At intensity 75-80% after 24-36 h	After 24-48 h	After 48-72 h	After 72-84 h

training. After a very intensive training session (with repeated efforts on an anaerobic level) recovery training is, in the first place, advisable. After a more moderate intensive session (training sessions around threshold) easy long endurance training of another discipline can be undertaken without any problems occurring. This training session must then again be followed by recovery training.

All the previous data shows that your training labor is only effective if sufficient (relative) recovery time is inserted after training to reach supercompensation.

What happens if the recovery time after training has not been sufficient becomes clear from the next diagram:

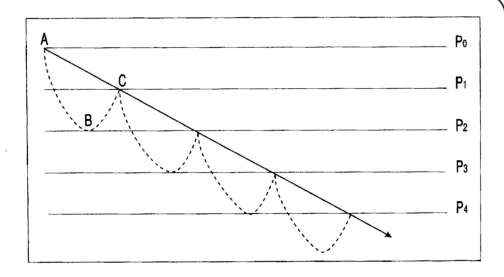

PO, P1, P2, P3, P4 ... *different performance levels*
AB: *drop of the performance level as a result of training fatigue*
BC: *the rise of the performance level during recovery period is insuffiently as a result of insufficient recovery time. A new training stimulus was inserted to early. As a result of this there is no supercompensation and we see a drop instead of a rise of performance level.*

The causes of overtraining often are situated outside training. For example: Successive races without sufficient chance for recovery, stress, insufficient sleep, infections, unbalanced diet, too little fluids, heat, jetlag, the use of certain medicines.

Often overtraining is caused by one of the factors mentioned above, which in its turn influences another factor: if you are mentally stressed you sleep less well, you process your training less well, your appetite diminishes, your energy balance becomes negative... If one thing goes wrong you will experience a whole chain of reactions.

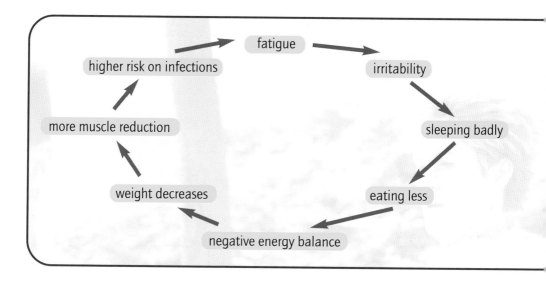

Recognizing overtraining

To avoid overtraining it is not only necessary to know the causes of overtraining, but also to have insight into the symptoms.

An important symptom of overtraining is a decrease in the maximum performance capacity. But there are still a lot of other indications. You'll also notice that your heart rate increases less rapidly than usual, and that you have to put in more effort than normal to increase your heart rate to a certain level. Often this is preceded by a period in which your resting heart rate also has increased. Recovery after effort is slowed down, although in some cases, in spite of overtraining, the heart rate rapidly drops after effort.

Furthermore there are still a number of mental indications of overtraining. You do not feel like training, you are irritable, you are not very hungry and you sleep poorly. In addition you have an increased risk of infection.

A specific example of the raised risk on infections is herpes. Herpes is a viral infection which often appears as cysts (also called fever blisters) on the lip or around the mouth. Once contaminated by it, the virus that causes herpes is always latently present in the body. During periods of reduced capacitance, for example when training too much, this infection breaks through.

You also notice that you are more susceptible to colds during periods of heavy training, or when you are in good shape. Colds are the consequence of contact with certain viruses. If the immune system against these viruses is weak, the odds of catching a cold increase. Research has proven that intensive training weakens the immune system. Hence athletes in top condition, after they have trained intensely, are more subject to these viruses.

Recognizing overtraining is often difficult, because a low heart rate during the effort and a fast recovery of the heart rate after the effort can be interpreted as positive training impact. Moreover, during a lactic acid test for possible overtraining, a reduced lactic acid quality during effort is established. This can also lead to misinterpretation.

To recognize overtraining, much attention must be paid to your mental state. Do you feel good, are you eager to train, do you have a normal sleeping pattern and a normal appetite, and do you process training smoothly? When you start to feel like you are in a training rut, it is advisable to stop training or scale back. A lot of scientists are convinced that overtraining is largely a mental issue. For this reason variations in training, and disruptions in training to pursue other entertainment not involving your sport are necessary.

It is also important to examine whether your heart rate obtains normal values during training. The heart rate which does not increase easily during training and therefore remains abnormally low in spite of increasing strain is often a sign that you are tired. It is again best to plan a recovery period.

In spite of all the previous observations, you cannot lose sight of the fact that you can be tired during a training session and a race without this necessarily implying overtraining. Before you can obtain positive training impact, you should be tired. It is, however, important that you insert sufficient recovery after efforts in order to reach supercompensation.

You should also distinguish overload from overtraining: In case of overload, fatigue disappears after a few days and you also will perform better after some recovery days.
In the case of overtraining, fatigue keeps on bugging you, even after some recovery days. Your performance level remains reduced.

Preventing overtraining

Determining overtraining is not simple, because at first sight you generally attribute a reduction of the performance level with too little training rather than too much training. Determining overtraining with certainty often happens late. The consequence is that you keep trying to catch up with the facts. It is also difficult to determine the cause of overtraining. For this reason there are a number of means to help you.

Keeping a training diary

In the training diary, the following issues are noted day after day: precise description of the kind of training done: duration, distance, intensity; How was training experienced (easy, tough...); How does recovery go?; Registration of the resting heart rate; Weight; Mental state; possibly other observations.

When there are symptoms of overtraining, you can consult the training diary and look for the beginning of the overtraining and possible causes.

Filling in a questionnaire

By daily filling in a questionnaire the risk on overtraining can be visualized:

QUESTIONNAIRE OVERTRAINING			
Date:...........			
Item	Score		
Training	1	2	3
Resting heart rate	1	2	3
Health	1	2	3
Sleep	1	2	3
Nutrition	1	2	3
Social	1	2	3
Stress	1	2	3
Total			

Explanation:

Example: 1 = excellent , 2 = average, could be better, 3 = bad

Training:
1 = training goes optimal,
feeling good while training
2 = training does not go really smoothly
3 = training is experienced as too tough,
the recovery does not go well

Resting heart rate: 1= normal morning pulse
2 = resting heart rate more than 10% higher
than usual
3 = morning pulse more than 15% higher
than usual

Health:
1 = feeling good, fit, healthy
2 = not 100% fit, not feeling good overall
3 = feeling bad, sick (never train)

Sleep:
1= excellent sleep
2 = sleep could be better
3 = disturbed sleep, often awake,
still tired in the morning

Nutrition:
1 = appetite is alright
2 = appetite is not optimal
3 = no appetite or strict diet

Social:
1= everything alright in the area relationships
(at home, school, boyfriend, girlfriend, work.)
2 = social contacts not optimal
3 = relational problems

Stress:
1 = feeling relaxed
2 = slightly stressed
3 = stressed, irritable, hot under the collar

For every item the score is indicated daily and the total is made. When scoring 1 for every item you obtain on that day a total of 7. The total score fluctuates between minimum 7 and maximum 21. Total of every daily score is presented in a graph.

If you see a rising line in the curve of the daily scores, the danger of overtraining exists. Then you can make an analysis of the causes of the increase of the curve and you can intervene before overtraining manifests itself.

CHAPTER 13

Overload injuries and how to avoid them

Overload injuries are a very annoying, but an almost inescapable consequence of regular and advanced training. It is dreaming of utopia to think that overload injuries can be completely avoided.

Running is a very straining sport, much more so than, for example, cycling and swimming.

While running, your body, and your feet in particular, need to absorb a great deal of shock. On average the pressure on the foot with every running step amounts to approximately three to four times the body weight. That is the reason why athletes who weigh more generally are more liable to injuries than lighter athletes.

As long as the strain and the resistance capacity of the movement system are in balance, there are no problems. Overload injuries arise when the training strain exceeds the capacity of the body.

Every runner has their own individual capacity. For inexperienced runners this capacity can be exceeded quickly. Much has to do with the familiarization of the body to the run training imposed. But even very experienced runners have to deal with the risk of overload injuries as well. In principle you could claim that a running volume of more than 60 kilometers per week implies potential risk of injuries for every runner, even for the most trained one.
An overload injury generally does not arise suddenly. Most of the time it is the eventual consequence of a process which has been going on for quite some time.

TIP:
Interrupt the training immediately in case of an injury. Continuing to train with pain generally results in a long-term convalescence period.

Causes of injuries

- **A wrong, too-quick training set-up**
  Your body needs time to adapt to an increasing strain. You must also take into account that the physiological adaptation of your body generally comes about more rapidly than the adaptation of your movement system. In other words, it is possible that a certain strain does not mean exaggerated strain for your heart, blood cycle and breathing system, but that your joints, tendons and muscles have not yet been sufficiently adapted to the training labor imposed.

- **A too-long, always increasing training strain without interruption by a rest period**
  One could more or less compare this situation to an elastic bandbeing stretched slowly further and further. This lasts till the elastic snaps.

- **A too-heavy, one-time workload**
  Generally an overload injury is the consequence of a long-term process, a repeated strain. An overload injury can, however, also arise immediately when suddenly exaggerated heavy effort is required, for example, when a marathon is being run without sufficient training background.

- **Deviations in putting your foot down**

- **Running on a hard surface**
  Too much running on a hard surface can cause a lot of misery to Achilles tendons, the shinbone and the knees. A soft surface softens the shock significantly.

- **Running with unsuitable shoes**

Common injuries

Overload injuries can differ greatly, and can arise in almost any spot in the movement system. In a lot of cases these injuries are inflammations of the tendons (tendinitis) in particular.

Inflammation is generally accompanied by the following symptoms: looking red, feels hot, swelling, pain (sensitive to pressure).

Tendinitis should first and foremost be treated using ice therapy. This means that you put ice on the spot which is inflamed. It often is advisable to massage the inflamed spot with a piece of ice, so the spot of the injury becomes cold through and through. This treatment is also called ice friction.

Generally you cannot do anything wrong when putting ice on an inflamed tendon. In a lot of cases it is the best way to control a the possibility of tendinitis without having to interrupt training entirely. In this case, the ice needs to be applied immediately after astrongly reduced effort, best for about 10 minutes, and several additional times a day. If the injury nevertheless gets worse, you should interrupt training completely and visit a sports doctor.

TIP:

Be careful that you do not "burn" the skin when applying ice friction due to the direct contact of the ice with the skin. That is why you would best apply a thin bandage around the ice.

Some common injuries for runners are tendinitis of the Achilles tendon, plantar fasciitis, periostitis and runner's knee.

Tendinitis of the Achilles tendon

The Achilles tendon is a very large, firm tendon which forms the connection between the calf muscles and the heel bone.

Generally this injury starts unsuspiciously, with a vaguely teasing feeling. In spite of this vague pain you can initially still keep on training. But here is where we meet the great risk. Often you still keep running until the pain forces you to stop training. In that case the tendon is most of the time swollen and sensitive to pressure.

Possible causes:
- Forcing up training too fast for too much training volume
- Running uphill
- Running on a hard surface
- Overpronation and oversupination of the foot, as a result of which the heel bone is being strained much more
- Running shoes with a bad heel which does not absorb shocks sufficiently
- Too short and rigid calf muscles, putting too much tension on the Achilles tendon
- Running in cold and wet weather conditions

Possible solutions:

- First of all, it is required to stop training. Chronic tendinitis of the Achilles tendon is very difficult to treat, because the tendon is not well supplied with blood. Complete immobilization by means of a plaster cast is the only option
- If the position of the feet is deviated, adapted soles can relieve the Achilles tendon
- A light raising of the heel
- Running shoes with adapted heel which absorb shocks better
- Stretching exercises for the calf muscles
- Running on a soft, but level surface
- Avoid running uphill
- Keep feet and Achilles tendons warm during running training sessions in cold and wet conditions
- Ice therapy

Runner's knee

Runner's knee is a term which includes a number of common knee injuries This high rate of injuries is not astonishing if you realize that the knee is a complicated joint through which two bones meet, namely the thigh bone and the shinbone. The calf bone is not a part of the knee joint. The knee joint further comprises the ligaments (6), the menisci (2) and the knee-cap (patella).

Factors which create a heavy strain on the knee are:

- Long-term strain
- High running speed
- Running on a hard surface
- A deviating foot position
- A deviating knee position
- Cycling with high resistance

The most common running injuries to the knee are:

Chondromalicia of the knee-cap

Chondromalicia is wear to the cartilage at the back of the knee-cap. The pain localizes itself at the front of the knee, over the complete joint. Running uphill and sitting with bended knees will worsen the pain.

Possible causes are:
- An instability of the joint
- A deviation of the feet. Both flat feet and hollow feet can cause the development of this injury

Possible solutions are:
- First of all, resting, followed by a gradual forcing-up of the training volume. The training sessions must be shortened in any case.
- Making the quadriceps stronger (front thigh muscle). This gives the knee more stability and there will be less wear of the cartilage.
- Checking if there is a deviated position of the feet. If the answer is yes, adapted soles can solve the problem since they correct the position during running.

Chondromalicia requires a swift diagnosis. Cartilage is a fabric that does not get well supplied with blood. That is why convalescence can be lengthy.

Inflammation of the iliotibial tractus

The iliotibial tractus is a tendon plate which runs along the outer part of the thigh and attaches it to the outer part of the under leg. When bending the knee this plate goes alongside the outer part of the knee over the femoral condyl. This is a projection of the lower part of the thigh bone.

When being overloaded at the topof this projection, friction causes inflammation. The pain arises during running, and can become so dramatic that you must stop running.

Possible causes are:
- Bowlegs
- A difference in leg length
- Oversupination of the foot
- Shortened or rigid muscles especially on the outer part of the thigh
- Too much running at the same side of a sloping road
- Too-fast training set-up
- Too much fast run training sessions

Possible solutions:
- Stretching the outer part of the thigh muscles regularly
- A good warm-up before every intensive run training session
- Running shoes which are adapted to the foot statics
- A good training set-up, with attention to gradually forcing up both the training volume and the training intensity

- Running on flat roads. If the road slants, you best vary the running direction regularly
- Apply ice immediately after the effort

Tendinitis of the patella tendon

The patella tendon (knee tendon) connects the knee-cap to the upper, front part of the shinbone. This knee tendon is the continuation of the four-headed thigh muscle (quadriceps femoris) that makes sure the knee can be stretched. Especially for jumping athletes, this tendon undergoes heavy pressure. That is why the injury in which the knee tendon is infected is also called a jumper's knee.

An inflammation of the patella tendon can, however, occur with runners and cyclists as well. Due to a long-term strain, the tendon gets irritated right below the joint. In serious cases the pain isn't just felt during running and cycling, but also when getting up in the morning.

Possible causes
- Running uphill too often
- Deviating position of the feet
- Too high and/or too rapid training set-up
- Too rigid and short hindmost thigh muscles (hamstrings)
- Too weak front thigh muscles, as a result of which the knee tendon is being strained too much

Possible solutions
- Scaling back of the training strain or undergoing a period of complete rest
- Running shoes which are adapted to the foot statics
- Avoid running uphill
- Stretching of the hindmost thigh muscles
- Very gradual and progressive reinforcement of the four-headed thigh muscle
- In case of inflammation: ice therapy

Plantar fasciitis

Under the foot sole there is a thick membrane that goes from the heel to the ball of the foot. This membrane gives support to the lower part of the foot. When too much pressure is put on this membrane, an inflammation can occur. The symptoms sometimes are pain in the complete lower part of the foot, sometimes only in the heel.

Often the pain is bearable in the beginning. If training is not interrupted, and if the cause of infection has not been removed the pain gets worse even to the extent that it becomes impossible to run any further.

This inflammation can turn out to be a very annoying, long-term injury when you keep on running with it too long. Swiftly interrupting training is a must.

Possible causes
- Too rapid increase of the training strain
- Running with insufficiently flexible soles
- Overpronation of the feet
- Flat feet

Possible solutions
- Immediately interrupting training when in pain
- Gradual training set-up
- Correct and high qualityshoe choice
- Adapted shoes in function of deviation of the foot
- Possible adaptation by wearing insoles

Shin splints

Shin splints arise when the pressure on the membrane covering the shinbone increases dramatically due to overload in the bottom third. Small tears in the membrane can occur. The pain can become so strong that continuing to run almost becomes impossible. Serious pain is experienced during shocks as each foot strikes the ground. There is also high sensitivity to pressure on the inner part of the lowportion of the shinbone.

Possible causes
- Running on hard surface
- Too abrupt transition from training on soft surface to training on hard surface
- Shoes with insufficient shock absorption
- Deviating position of the feet

Possible solutions:
- Interrupting training
- Running on soft surface
- Gradual switching from training on soft surface to training on hard surface
- Adapted running shoes with good shock absorption

CHAPTER 14

Medical support

Blood parameters

First of all, a medical check-up at the start of a new training advancement is really useful. By this we mean a general medical check-up, a cardiac check during an effort test (every two years) and a blood check-up, which is best repeated every three to four months. By means of this blood check-up, certain shortages can be established and you can find out if you should take supplements.

Some important blood parameters which directly or indirectly influence your performance are:

- **The red blood cells (RBC):**

The RBC transport oxygen in the body. A high number of RBC is therefore favorable for a runner. Experience teaches that after a period of tough training sessions or races, the number of RBC often decreases. After a recovery period, an increase should occur. A fall in number of RBC can be an indication to scale back the training volume.

- **Hemoglobin:**

Hemoglobin is a protein that links itself with oxygen. A high hemoglobin quality is therefore of interest to athletes because the oxygen transport rises. This quality is also affected by overly tough training sessions.

- **The haematocrite:**

This is the proportion of the number of RBC with respect to the total blood volume. For this reason, high haematocrite value indicates a high oxygen transport capacity, which is also very interesting for a athlete.

- **Creatine kinase (CK):**

CK is an enzyme that indicates muscle reduction. Overly intensive training sessions or insufficient recovery between the training sessions and/or races lead to a high CK-value. High CK-value is an absolute indication to reduce the training intensity.

- **Urea:**

Urea is a substance released when proteins are demolished. A too high urea level in athletes can indicate that too little fluid is taken in during and after the training sessions.

- **Testosterone:**

Testosterone is an anabolic (constructive) hormone. A fall in testosterone levels can indicate that the body is no longer processing your training. Reducing the training strain, both quantitatively and qualitatively, is strongly advisable in this case.

- **Cortisol:**

Cortisol is a catabolic (demolishing) hormone. An increase in cortisol levels indicates that training is no longer processed well. The proportion of testosterone to cortisol is also important. Fall of testosterone level and simultaneous increase of the cortisol level is an indication that the runner is not recuperating sufficiently.

- **Vitamin B12 and folic acid:**

Vitamin B12 and folic acid are needed to build proteins and RBC.

- **Ferritine:**

Ferritine is a protein iron complex which determines the iron reserve in the body. Iron is needed for the production of RBC and hemoglobin. A shortage of iron decreases hemoglobin levels and the number of RBC.

- **Magnesium:**

Magnesium is an important factor in energy metabolism and influences the nerve muscle sensitivity. Shortage of magnesium manifests itself clinically by a disturbed nerve muscle function (among other things cramps) and muscle weakness.

Altitude training

The parameters above show that the number of red blood cells is an important element in the performance capacity of the athlete.

A natural means to multiply this number is altitude training. At a certain altitude the body adapts to the reduced atmospheric pressure by producing new red blood cells.

The conditions for good altitude training are: a stay at an altitude of more than 1500m for at least 3 weeks.

In practice at altitude, your training period must be subdivided into a number of phases. **Phase 1** is the acclimatization phase, which is needed for the body to adapt to altitude. On average this phase takes 3 to 5 days. In the beginning of this phase there is a clearly raised resting heart rate. Your normal training volume must consciously be scaled back until your resting heart rate has reached its normal value.

Phase 2 takes 5 days. Training volume is progressively forced up, emphasizing clearly training volume and not training intensity. You only do easy aerobic training sessions.

Phase 3 – During the third phase you can train intensively. Do not forget however that the body recovers more slowly from efforts made at altitude. You should pay more attention to the recovery phase after training than at sea level.

When returning to sea level you should take a few important guidelines into account. The first 10 days after returning to sea level are necessary to adapt again to the new situation. During this phase the emphasis is on lighter, easy training sessions. This phase is a supercompensation phase to maximally profit from the effects of the past altitude training. Afterwards you reach a stage of increased performance level. Especially during the third week after returning to sea level are said to be ideal to achieve top performances.

But not all studies univocally emphasize the positive impact of altitude training, because

- The maximum heart rate decreases by 1% per 400m altitude
- The maximum oxygen intake capacity decreases by 10% per 1000m, starting to count from 1200m
- To reach the same performance as at sea level, more carbohydrates are consumed at altitude
- Speed with which lactic acid is removed has slowed down
- When training at altitude, recovery has slowed down
- By the fall of the plasma volume, the increase of the number of RBC and hemoglobin is only relative
- The quality of the RBC has decreased
- Generally speaking the athlete sleeps less well during an altitude training period
- The appetite diminishes in comparison with sea level
- At altitude there is a higher risk of dehydration

Sometimes you can opt for other procedures to get round these disadvantages, namely training at altitude and sleeping at sea level, or training at sea level and sleeping at altitude Especially this last procedure is said to be most effective. The research results on this are however not certified.

Photos and illustration credits

Cover design: Jens Vogelsang, Germany

Cover photo: Octagon CIS/Bob Verbeeck

Inside photos: Octagon CIS/Bob Verbeeck, Polar Electro GmbH, getty images, imago Sportfotodienst